Contents

Acknowledgments	*ix*
Introduction	*xi*

Kurt Angle	1
"Stone Cold" Steve Austin	6
Chris Benoit	14
The Big Show	18
Booker T	23
Christian	27
Diamond Dallas Page	30
The Dudley Boyz	33
Edge	37
Ric Flair	42
Mick Foley	47
The Hardy Boyz	51
Chris Jericho	58
Kane	65
Lita	71
The McMahons	78
Raven	87
William Regal	93
Rhyno	100

Contents

Rikishi   106
The Rock   110
Saturn   116
Al Snow   122
Lance Storm   128
Trish Stratus   132
Tajiri   136
Tazz   139
Triple H   142
The Undertaker   149
Rob Van Dam   155

How to Become a Professional Wrestler   **163**
*Find out where to go so you too can one day become
a monster of the mat.*

The Real Deal   **177**
An extensive list of wrestlers' real names.

The History of WrestleMania   **180**
Get the inside scoop on the Super Bowl of wrestling.

Wrestling Glossary   **205**
*Check out the real meaning behind some of
the most popular wrestling terms.*

Acknowledgments

Writing a book can be a very daunting task, but when you are surrounded by so many great people in your life, the task becomes that much easier. One of the first people that comes to mind for me is my editor, Kelly Sinanis. Words cannot express how much her vision and guidance helps me when it comes time to put the words on the page. She is a master at her craft. Her patience and understanding through what was a trying time in my life was also much appreciated.

Steve Ciacciarelli was also very instrumental with helping me get this book off the ground. His wrestling knowledge and insight is unrivaled in the rough and tough industry, and without his help *Monsters of the Mat* would still be a thought as opposed to a finished work. Next on my list of thanks are my lensmen, Jeff Eisenberg, Howard Kernats, and BlackJack Brown. Without their great material this book would just be a bunch of words.

My coworkers over at NHL Ice—Phil Coffey, Rich Libero, Shawn Roarke, Doug Karda, Russ Levine, Roger Sackaroff, Darryl Haberman, Matt Rogers, John McGourty, and Keith Ritter—I can't thank them enough for their support and making work a fun place to be every day.

And last but not least, I can't thank my family and friends enough. Mom and Dad, you two are the rock that I lean upon for support every day of my life. Charles and William, I couldn't ask for two better people to have as brothers. The two of you are truly

Acknowledgments

amazing. William, Rose, Deanna, Danielle, Ariana, and Nicole, whenever I see any of you I smile because I know the future of our family is in good hands. Diane, Penny, Uncle Ralph, Aunt Mitch, Bart and Fay, know that even though we were all born of different blood, I still have a special place in my heart for all of you. Aunt Kat and the entire Cassiliano clan, thanks for your love and support. Know that I love you all very much.

To Nick and Marie Silvestro, thank you for not only making me feel welcome in your home and family from day one, but also thank you for allowing me to marry your beautiful daughter, Denise, who I love more than life itself. Denise, you are not only the air that I breathe, but also my future.

And as always, a kiss up to my eyes in the sky; each of you is always on my mind and in my heart.

x

Introduction

O ver the years, every form of entertainment has had its share of performers who have transcended their industry. They not only become household names, but larger-than-life icons. Fans all over the world adore them, imitate them, and watch their every move. Movie stars like John Wayne, Marilyn Monroe, Clark Gable, Robert DeNiro, Brad Pitt, Al Pacino, and Julia Roberts fall into this category. Frank Sinatra, The Beatles, Elvis, Madonna—these entertainers' names are all synonymous with idols, legends, and superstars.

The same holds true in pro sports. Every basketball fan grows up yearning to someday "be like Mike"—the legendary Michael Jordan, that is. Every hockey, baseball, football, golf, or boxing fan may want to grow up and become Wayne Gretzky, Babe Ruth, John Elway, Tiger Woods, or Muhammad Ali.

The pro wrestling circuit has also had its share of stars. Monsters of the mat like Hulk Hogan, "Rowdy" Roddy Piper, Andre the Giant, George "The Animal" Steele, Bruno Sammartino, the Fabulous Moolah, "Superstar" Billy Graham, Ric Flair, and Terry Funk have all paved the way for modern-day ring leaders, including The Rock, "Stone Cold" Steve Austin, Triple H, The Undertaker, Kane, Booker T, Kurt Angle, Lita, Rob Van Dam, Chris Jericho, and a whole slew of others.

Whether heel or hero, friend or foe, these rulers of the ring bring something other than their God-given skills to the table each night, keeping the fans coming to the arena or tuned to their TV sets in record numbers. In the past few years, these leaders of sports-entertainment have been raking in millions of dollars from their outlandish live arena performances and their top TV shows, including Monday Night Raw, which has routinely outdrawn popular sports shows like Monday Night Football. Wrestling programs like WWF SmackDown! and MTV's *WWF Tough Enough* have become champions in the prime-time ratings war and have found a loyal following that tunes in each week to find out what's going to happen next in the wild and wacky world of pro wrestling.

But this unique brand of entertainment hasn't only found success on the small screen. The motion picture industry has also tapped into the wrestling world talent, calling on federation stars such as The Rock, Diamond Dallas Page, Hulk Hogan, "Rowdy" Roddy Piper, Sting, Goldberg, Mick Foley, Terry Funk, and countless others to make movie magic in films like *Ready to Rumble, No Holds Barred, Beyond the Mat, They Live, The Mummy Returns,* and *The Scorpion King.*

These squared-circle giants have also hit the mainstream market by gracing the covers and pages of popular publications such as *TV Guide, Sports Illustrated, Newsweek, Entertainment Weekly, USA Today, Vanity Fair, Vibe, Premiere, Playboy,* and *People.* The monsters have also had their mugs appear on shows such as *Saturday Night Live, Star Trek: Voyager,* the MTV Video Music Awards, the Grammy Awards, *Nash Bridges, The Tonight Show with Jay Leno, Martha Stewart Living,* MTV's *Total Request Live,* the *Howard Stern Show, Pacific Blue, Third Rock from the Sun,* and *Thunder in Paradise,* which just so happens to have been Hulk Hogan's own action-adventure show.

Like Godzilla and King Kong before them, these entertainment giants cannot be contained. They are reaching levels previously unknown to your common actor or athlete. These monsters yield to nothing—and nobody. In this ultimate A–Z guide, *Monsters of the Mat* manages to contain all of today's hottest ring kings and queens. It has all the wild world champions, the cunning contenders, hungry up-and-comers, and demons of destruction. This supreme fan guide also contains an in-depth look at some of the top wrestling schools in the country and takes a look back at the birth of the Super Bowl of wrestling—WrestleMania. As an added bonus, there's also a glossary of wrestling terms and a section on wrestlers' real names.

So instead of opening up a can of whoop ass on your favorite foe, open a copy of *Monsters of the Mat,* and get ready to rumble with some of the biggest superstars in sports-entertainment!

Kurt Angle

When Kurt Angle won his first World Wrestling Federation championship on October 22, 2000, at No Mercy, beating out The Rock, there's a good chance that his tears of joy weren't all that real. But if you flash back four years from his first WWF title win to the Summer Olympics in Atlanta, where Angle won an Olympic gold medal in the 220-pound weight class of freestyle wrestling, you'll find out his tears were quite genuine.

The impressive victory over Abbas Jadidi of Iran capped off a run for the Pennsylvania native that was both mentally and physically taxing. Angle trained long and hard for the chance to be the best in the world. He also overcame many obstacles, including a serious neck injury and the death of his mentor, Dave Schultz, who was murdered right before Angle was to compete in Georgia.

In order to take part in the Summer Games and have the best chance of winning, Angle knew he needed to train full-time, which left him no time to earn a paycheck. His mother, Marie, immediately took him back and showed her support by allowing her son to live with her while he got good and ready for the ultra-competitive games.

But several months before Angle, who was a two-time NCAA Division I National Champion and three-time All-American at Clarion University, was to compete in the tournament of his life, his world was turned upside down. His trainer and good friend, Dave Schultz, was murdered in January '96 on the estate of billionaire John du Pont. A grief-stricken Angle was forced to dig down deep inside and somehow find the strength to continue his quest for the gold.

As if that weren't enough strain on him, two and a half months before the Games, the medal hopeful severely injured his neck in the United States Nationals, putting in jeopardy his chances of going to Atlanta as a member of the U.S. team. It took several doctors and the same diagnosis each time (cracked vertebra, four pulled muscles, and two bulging disks) to make Angle take seriously their suggestions of six months of rest and not competing in the Olympics.

But he ignored the doctors orders anyway, and Angle went to the Olympic Trials where he won the tourney on sheer guts, will, and determination, which placed him in a better frame of mind for the Summer Games. The baby-faced wrestler rolled through his matches with ease at the Olympic Games in Atlanta, setting up a memorable finals match on July 31, 1996, against a real-life heel-of-a-wrestler, Abbas Jadidi, who hailed from Iran.

The two Olympians went at each other tooth and nail that night, necessitating an eight-minute overtime session to try and decide a winner. When neither grappler stepped to the forefront in the OT period to claim the prize, the decision as to who was going to walk away with the gold was left up to the Olympic officials.

When the referee stepped between the two finalists to announce his decision, Jadidi was so confident that he had won that he raised his arm in victory even before the ref opened his mouth. To his surprise, it was Angle's arm that was raised and Angle was declared the winner, sending the Iranian wrestler into a tizzy.

As for the American victor, it proved to be one of the most emotional experiences of his life. Not only did Angle grab hold of an American flag and run around the arena leading the crowd in chants of "USA," he also cried his eyes out on the podium when the gold medal was placed around his neck and the national anthem was played.

"I just let go," Angle explained at a press conference afterward. "I was just thinking about how hard I trained and how much stress I went through to do this."

Without having visions of becoming a pro wrestler at the time, he scoffed at Vince McMahon's initial offer to work for the WWF immediately following his golden win.

But the Olympic hero would come around to the WWF two years later after trying his hand at sportscasting and motivational speaking. He inked a five-year deal with the Connecticut-based wrestling organization in October 1998, and the newly signed warrior was immediately shipped out to learn the professional way of wrestling from Dory Funk, Jr., at his Funkin' Dojo, the wrestling school that he ran for the WWF.

When other former Olympic and amateur wrestlers began questioning Angle's job choice, claiming he sold his wrestling soul to the devil for a chance at fame and fortune, the new WWFer replied by saying: "I don't look at this as a step up or down. It's a new career and it's only going to help my sport, which has been in the shadows too long. They don't even call it pro wrestling anymore; it's sports and entertainment."

He first "angled" in 1999 in the WWF as the only "real athlete" on the circuit, which immediately stirred the pot in the promotion and got under the skin of some veteran grapplers. He made his Pay-Per-View debut on November 14, 1999, at the Survivor Series in Detroit, Michigan. The newcomer took on and defeated Shawn Stasiak, which didn't go over too well with the jam-packed crowd, who immediately started booing the Olympic hero. When he heard the jeers Angle couldn't believe his golden ears. He grabbed the mic and reminded the fans that they shouldn't be booing an Olympic gold medalist, which only riled them up even more.

Angle gave the fans plenty more to boo about during his rookie season, as he not only won the European and Intercontinental titles, he also walked away with the King of the Ring crown in 2000 after only being on the circuit for less than six months. He won the Euro title on February 8, 2000, against Val Venis during a SmackDown! taping in Austin, Texas. The 6-foot-2, 220-pound patriot also won the Intercontinental strap three weeks later in Hartford, Connecticut, when he downed Chris Jericho at No Way Out. He then became WWF King on June 25, 2000, when he gave the over-400-pound Rikishi a belly-to-belly suplex off the top rope.

But Angle really shocked the wrestling world that year when he garnered the World Championship from "The People's Champion," The Rock, at the Pepsi Arena in Albany, New York, at No Mercy, becoming the fastest rising star in the history of the World Wrestling Federation.

The two superstars battled it out in a No Disqualification match for the prestigious title strap, where Stephanie McMahon and Rikishi both played devious roles when they interfered in the contest at different times. Stephanie, who accompanied Angle to the ring that night, tried to distract the Brahma Bull so the former Olympic champion could win his first heavyweight title. Rikishi entered the scene, supposedly on the side of The Rock, but ended up helping Angle when he accidentally hit the third-generation wrestler with a super kick. Angle took advantage of the miscue and nailed both big stars with Olympic Slams, ultimately pinning The Rock and winning the right to be called WWF Champion.

Over the course of his short WWF career, Angle has not only been the holder of other prestigious belts such as the WCW World title, the WWF Hardcore title, WWF King of the Ring, and the WCW United States title, he has also tussled with some of the most talented grapplers on the pro circuit, including Triple H, The Rock, "Stone Cold" Steve Austin, Chris Jericho, Chris Benoit, The Undertaker, Booker T, Rikishi, Rob Van Dam, and Kane. But the American battler doesn't intend on stopping there. Kurt Angle will take on any and all who dare to stand in his way as he believes he's the only "true" athlete in the business.

Like The Rock, Chyna, Mick Foley, and Diamond Dallas Page, Angle also tackled the wrestling book world when he penned his autobiography, *It's True! It's True!*, in 2001. The former amateur grappling great chronicles his success story in the 317-page work, escorting the reader through his lifelong journey from Olympic hero to WWF superstar. There is just no stopping this talented wrestler.

"Stone Cold" Steve Austin

Despite being known as a "rattlesnake," the meanest S.O.B. in wrestling, and a hell-raiser, "Stone Cold" Steve Austin still remains one of the most popular wrestlers in the world today.

The fans truly adore this blue-collar grappler who comes to the ring each and every night with a kick-ass attitude, ready to rumble with anybody who dares to get in his way—including his boss. Almost from the very beginning of his WWF career, Austin has made it quite clear to his friends, foes, and fans that he doesn't need anyone or any gimmick in order to have success on the mat.

World Wrestling Federation owner Vince McMahon knew he had his hands full when the former WCWer came on the scene with long, flowing blond locks and began trash-talking the federation's head honcho even before he even stepped one foot between the ropes in 1995. As soon as he learned of the "Ring Master" character that McMahon wanted him to portray, the loudmouth brawler knocked heads with his new boss. This, unbeknownst to either of them, was a sign of things to come.

Not only did Austin feel uncomfortable about playing this "Ring Master" role, who he felt belonged under a circus big top rather than a wrestling ring, he also didn't like sharing the spotlight with anyone else. At the time, McMahon had his new employee under the management of "Million Dollar Man" Ted DiBiase, which didn't sit well with the solitary wrestler.

Less than a year later the duo would part ways under "suspicious circumstances" as the Ring Master lost a stipulations match to Savio Vega on May 16, 1996, during a WWF Pay-Per-View event. The "questionable factors" of the match had to do with the stipulations, which not only called for the two wrestlers to be linked together by a leather leash, but also the Master agreed that if he lost to Vega, DiBiase would have to leave the federation.

After Vega defeated his opponent in the match, rumors swirled in and around the federation that the Ring Master threw the bout so he could rid himself of his useless manager and also put the character gimmick to bed. While Austin never will admit to losing on purpose, he did have this to say at the time of the loss to Vega and the subsequent departure of DiBiase: "I never needed nobody to do the talkin' for me and I certainly didn't need some suit telling me who I should or shouldn't be challenging. That went for Ted and it goes for everybody on down."

With the "Million Dollar Man" and the Ring Master now a thing of the past, the 6-foot-2, 252-pound gladiator now looked to the future. The superstar-in-the-making would now be seen kicking ass and taking numbers on the WWF circuit as "Stone Cold" Steve Austin, a goateed grappler complete with a bald head, chiseled frame, and a monster attitude.

"Stone Cold" had his coming out party on June 23, 1996, at a King of the Ring event, when he not only made himself famous by kicking Jake "The Snake" Roberts's butt in front of a sold-out crowd, but he also coined the infamous "Austin 3:16" phrase that night.

After knocking off Marc Mero in the semifinal match of the King of the Ring event, "Stone Cold" took on and defeated the Bible-thumping Roberts, who was famous for his religious psalm references, with his now famous finishing move, the "Stone Cold" Stunner. Austin also grabbed the mic so he could add insult to "The Snake's" injured pride.

In front of the entire wrestling world, Austin brought down the house and Roberts when he said: "You talk about your psalms. You talk about John 3:16. Well, Austin 3:16 says I just whipped your ass!"

Thus creating a legend and million-dollar catchphrase all at once.

While this ad-libbed incident put "Stone Cold" over with the WWF fans and management, causing an insane run on Austin merchandise, the hungry wrestler wanted more than fame and fortune—he wanted championship gold! His wins over Mero and Roberts were an impressive start to the climb up the WWF ladder, but he knew there were much bigger challenges ahead of him and he didn't care who he had to knock over to get there.

After taking on and defeating grapplers such as Yokozuna and Hunter Hearst Helmsley, Austin wanted a piece of the federation's top dog, Bret "The Hitman" Hart. "Stone Cold" didn't care that

Hart was the owner of numerous WWF titles, he only knew that he was considered the best at the time. Austin knew that if he wanted to be the best, he would have to knock off the guy who claimed to be "the best there is, the best there was, and the best there ever will be."

The two locked horns many times over the course of their careers, with their first clash coming at the 1996 Survivor Series in New York City's Madison Square Garden. While "The Hitman" got the best of "Stone Cold" on this night, it would only be the beginning of what became an all-out war between the two WWF superstars. One of the most impressive matches of Austin's career came in 1997 in an "I quit" match against Hart at WrestleMania 13.

The "I quit" stipulation of the bout was inserted so that one wrestler had to utter the submission phrase in order for the other grappler to be determined the winner. Heading into the WrestleMania contest, Austin vowed that he would never utter the phrase "I quit" to Hart and he held true to his words, even though he lost the match.

The rock 'em sock 'em match saw both wrestlers take a pounding from each other with Hart ultimately trapping Austin in his lethal Sharpshooter hold in an attempt to get the bloody "Stone Cold" to say the magic words. But the determined wrestler stuck to his guns and instead of submitting to Hart, he passed out "stone cold," leaving Hart once again victorious.

One month later, Austin took on and defeated Hart in another clash of the WWF titans, but he wasn't satisfied with the win because he won by disqualification. This not only left "Stone Cold" stewing, it also set up a rematch between the two the following night on a RAW telecast.

In a No Holds Barred match in front of a worldwide television audience, Austin would finally beat Hart fair and square. But the good old-fashioned ass-whopping Austin put on "The Hitman" that night turned ugly when "Stone Cold" went psycho on Hart, who was taken away in an ambulance. Austin somehow managed to sneak into the emergency vehicle and continued to lay the smackdown on his helpless foe, causing Hart to miss the next three months of ring action.

Austin's battle with "The Hitman" eventually turned into a family affair, as "Stone Cold" waged war against the entire Hart Foundation. The epic battles led to him not only getting revenge on his foes, but also to his winning his first WWF championship gold. On May 27, 1997, Austin teamed up with another federation superstar, Shawn Michaels, against the reigning tag-team champions, Owen Hart and the British Bulldog, and the duo snagged the belts right out from under the champions' noses.

This win started a vicious battle between Austin and the younger Hart, which almost cost "Stone Cold" his livelihood. At the 1997 SummerSlam event at the Meadowlands in New Jersey, the two went toe-to-toe for Hart's Intercontinental title, which Austin would win for his first WWF singles title—but not without paying a steep price.

During the match, Hart attempted a piledriver on his opponent and Austin hit his head on the canvas awkwardly, subsequently breaking his neck. While the missed move caused the serious neck injury to "Stone Cold," the tough-as-nails grappler continued on and somehow managed to finish off his foe for the pin, win, and belt that night.

He stayed out of ring action for quite some time that year, but still managed to show up on occasion, stirring the pot wherever and whenever he could, especially at Owen Hart matches. Then finally, Austin got revenge on his rival at the 1997 Survivor Series, where the two once again squared off for the IC belt.

The bald battler again came away with the belt proving not only to his competitor that he was all the way back from his severe injury, but also to the entire wrestling nation. While the IC belt was a nice way to stage a comeback in the federation, it wasn't quite what Austin had in mind when he got into the business. He wanted more. He wanted to live his golden dreams.

After defending his strap against a hungry up-and-comer called The Rock, "Stone Cold" decided that he had bigger fish to fry and relinquished his belt to the young WWF wrestler. His sights were now set on the top of the WWF mountain—the heavyweight championship!

With WWF gold now on his mind, "Stone Cold" entered the 1998 Royal Rumble and came away with a hard-fought victory over The Rock, after an intense battle in the thirty-man free-for-all tournament, making him the undisputed number one contender for Shawn Michaels' championship title.

The two former tag partners would clash for the right to be called WWF champ at WrestleMania XIV in Boston and the Texas Rattlesnake would come out on top, giving him his first-ever World Wrestling Federation Championship.

This title change didn't make Vince McMahon very happy because he didn't want a beer-guzzling, bird-flipping, out-of-control wrestler sitting atop his wrestling federation, so he tried to lure his champion over to the corporate side. Austin almost had McMahon and the wrestling audience fooled when one night he showed up in the ring alongside his boss all decked out in a suit and tie on an episode of RAW. But a few minutes into the "business" meeting, Austin shed his corporate skin and delivered his patented "Stone Cold" Stunner to his boss, sending the crowd into a frenzy. On that night, Austin made it perfectly clear to his boss and the audience that he would never go corporate. "Stone Cold" was only interested in one business and one business only—the ass-kicking business!

This unique wrestling feud went over really well with the audience, as Austin became a modern-day cult hero because of his constant willingness to take on, defeat, and embarrass his boss. While the two have clashed hot and heavy over the years, no one battle was more embarrassing for McMahon than the time "Stone Cold" held a fake weapon to his head honcho's cranium, causing the grown man to soil his custom-made suit.

Throughout his time in the WWF, the talented grappler has won his share of titles in the federation. In his career Austin has won the World Wrestling Federation Championship six times; the Intercontinental belt two times; the tag straps four times; King of the Ring once; and is a three-time Royal Rumble winner.

Austin has also tangled with sports-entertainment's best such as Kurt Angle, Triple H, Mankind, The Undertaker, Rikishi, Kane, Chris Benoit, D'Lo Brown, Shane McMahon, William Regal, Booker T, Rhyno, and countless others.

He has been known to do whatever it takes to get to the top of the wrestling mountain, even if it means changing allegiances or federations to do so. And that's exactly what "Stone Cold" did on July 22, 2001, in Cleveland, Ohio.

The WWF's hell-raiser sure did raise some hell and eyebrows on this night in the sold-out Gund Arena when he turned his back on the federation and jumped ship to the WCW/ECW side of the wrestling world, helping them win the Inaugural Brawl at the properly named Invasion event.

The historic match featured five wrestlers from Team WWF taking on five wrestlers from Team WCW/ECW for wrestling world bragging rights. The WWF squad was made up of Austin, Kurt Angle, Chris Jericho, The Undertaker, and Kane, while the WCW/ECW crew consisted of Diamond Dallas Page, Booker T, Rhyno, and the Dudley Boyz.

Just when it looked like Angle was going to put it away for Team

WWF, as he had Booker T in an Ankle Lock submission, Austin came in and broke his teammate's hold and surprisingly nailed him with a Stunner. In the process, he also rolled Booker onto the fallen Angle and ordered the ref to count out Angle and the WWF, thereby selling out his federation.

While it very well may have been a shock to Vince McMahon and his WWF teammates, Austin's actions should not have been a surprise to the wrestling world. "Stone Cold" has always been about himself. He is a loner. His only drive is winning championships and he'll do whatever it takes to keep himself in line for the belts, even if it means turning his back on his so-called friends. He proved that in July 2001 when he turned his back on the WWF at Invasion to help Team WCW/ECW get the victory over Team WWF. Just remember, this guy didn't get the nickname "Rattlesnake" for being a loyal and friendly guy.

The man who often uses the phrase DTA (don't trust anyone) lives by his own words, and those around him should take heed because this brawny brawler has no intention of changing. He has won countless titles by being a mean fighting machine and he'll continue to do so until *he* feels like stopping.

What the future holds for this bad-to-the-bone wrestler only the wrestling gods know for sure, but you can bet your very last dollar that Steve Austin will compete for whatever title he wants, whenever he wants " 'cause 'Stone Cold' said so."

Chris Benoit

Chris Benoit is about as plain as they come in the wrestling world. He doesn't come to the ring with any bells and whistles, nor does he don any outlandish costumes or grapple with gimmicks in the ring. But if you're going to view a WWF event either live or on the tube when Benoit is on the card, get your popcorn early because you're not going to want to miss any of his high-flying, powerful maneuvers.

The straight-as-an-arrow gladiator comes to the ring packing only his chiseled frame and a wrestling arsenal that's surely second to none on the modern-day circuit. He's not into all that glitz and glamour like the other top-notch performers. He is only interested in pounding and pummeling his opponents, while also picking up a few titles along the way for good measure and memories.

Before becoming a World Wrestling Federation star, the Montreal native trained in the world-famous Dungeon in Calgary under the tutelage of Stu Hart and his sons. His training with the Harts not only afforded him the opportunity to become one of the best technical wrestlers in the history of sports-entertainment, it also gave him an opportunity to see the world. During his career, Benoit wrestled all throughout Europe, Japan, and North America before ever stepping one boot in either the WWF, WCW, or ECW.

The Canadian Crippler made his pro debut in Stampede Wrestling in December 1985, when he was one half of a tag team with Rich Patterson against Karl Moffat and Mike Hammer. The newly formed tag squad not only impressed the crowd and their foes that night in Canada, they also left the ring victorious, starting the brilliant career of one of today's most gifted grapplers off on the right foot.

Three months later the star-on-the-rise would get his first taste of gold when he again joined up with a ring partner, Ben Bassarab, to take on another tag tandem. Together, the B&B boys took out their foes, Ron Starr and Wayne Farris, on March 1, 1986, in Regina, Saskatchewan, to earn the right to be called tag-team champions.

A little over two months later, Benoit teamed with Keith Hart to win the International Tag Team title over the Cuban Assassin and Farris on May 9, 1986. From there the green grappler left for Japan where he would stay and earn a living in the New Japan promotion for the majority of 1987.

He returned to Calgary and Hart's Stampede promotion in 1988 and won the International Tag Team titles two more times along with several other British Commonwealth straps. When Stampede dimmed its lights on the wrestling world for the last time in December 1989, Benoit was again on the move—this time jet-setting to countries such as Japan, Mexico, and Germany.

While his time overseas surely shaped his game, it was his time spent in the ECW and WCW that really got him ready to rumble with the best-of-the-best in the WWF. ECW allowed Benoit to not only hone his technical skills, but the Philadelphia-based federation also allowed him to add some edge to his character. He found out soon enough that the ECW didn't have the word "extreme" in its title for nothing.

His time with the WCW afforded him the opportunity to not only tackle such opponents as Bret Hart, Diamond Dallas Page, Saturn, Booker T, Jeff Jarrett, Kevin Sullivan, and Sid Vicious, it also gave him a chance to wear WCW gold several times before heading to the WWF.

On January 31, 2000, Benoit, Saturn, Eddie Guerrero, and Dean Malenko all showed up sitting ringside at a RAW cablecast during a match between Steve Blackman, Al Snow, and the New Age Outlaws. During the memorable match, the Road Dogg ventured out into the audience and attacked the former WCWers, prompting the four men to go on the attack against the WWF stars.

Benoit and company proved that night that they wouldn't be intimidated by anyone in the federation. As a matter of fact, the 5-foot-10, 220-pound wrestler took on most of the WWF's elite in his first three months on the scene. He first took on the federation's champion at the time, Triple H, and gradually moved his way down the ladder and tussled with stars like The Rock, Chris Jericho, Kane, Tazz, Test, and Rikishi.

More impressively, this talented gladiator won his first WWF championship strap after being on the circuit for less than 120 days. In stunning fashion, the former WCW heavyweight champion won his first title at WrestleMania 2000 in Anaheim, California, in a two-fall, Triple Threat match with Chris Jericho and Kurt Angle where both the Intercontinental and European championships were on the line. The first fall would decide the IC winner, while the second would determine the Euro champ.

Benoit not only walked out of the ring that night the newly crowned IC champ, he also sent a loud and clear message to all the WWF talent and fans, making it evident that he didn't come to the federation for fame or fortune, but rather to win championships.

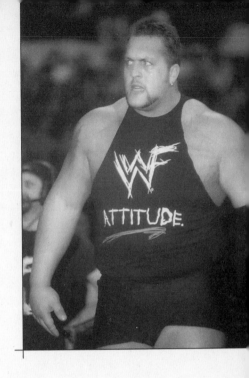

The Big Show

The Big Show has been riding on the wild and wacky ride of professional wrestling for seven years now and it's safe to say that his career has seen more ups and downs than the world-famous Cyclone roller coaster on a hot summer day on New York's Coney Island.

The Big Show, who came on the World Championship Wrestling circuit in July 1995 at the tender age of twenty-four, made a huge splash on the entire grappling nation in October of the same year when he took on the world's most famous wrestler, Hulk Hogan. The WCW wisely coined their newest warrior The Giant, as they tried to push him off as the long-lost son of the legendary wrestler, Andre the Giant.

The full-bodied freshman gladiator tried to take advantage of the hype and opportunities that the federation placed before him by not only besting Hogan by disqualification at Halloween Havoc in Detroit's Joe Louis Arena, but by also aligning himself with the Dungeon of Doom. Even though he beat the wrestling icon by DQ, it didn't matter to the new wrestler, as he had just won his first WCW world title after only being on the circuit for three short months.

Three months later, the rookie met up with another monster of the mat, "Nature Boy" Ric Flair. The duo took on and beat Hulk Hogan and "Macho Man" Randy Savage at Clash of Champions on January 23, 1996, in Las Vegas, Nevada, when Flair pinned Savage to the canvas nine minutes and fifty-one seconds into the contest.

Six months after his debut, The Giant would meet up again with Flair, but this time they wouldn't be on the same side. On April 22, 1996, in Albany, Georgia, the young wrestler was about to take on the stylin' and profilin' veteran for his second shot at winning a world championship. Once again the 7-foot-1 competitor, who was trained by Larry Sharpe, would shock the WCW fans by beating another ruler of the ring with his deadly chokeslam. The Giant held onto that title until Road Wild that summer, when the Hulkster got his revenge on the upstart wrestler from Tampa, Florida, on August 10, 1996, in Sturgis, San Diego.

Because of his first-year successes, The Giant was voted the 1996 *Pro Wrestling Illustrated* Rookie and Wrestler of the Year, and became one of the biggest stars in all of wrestling.

The Giant would also strike WCW gold on the tag-team circuit, winning three tag straps with three different teammates. He would win his first tag title paired with Lex Luger at WCW's SuperBrawl VII in San Francisco, California. The duo bested The Outsiders (Kevin Nash and Scott Hall) on February 23, 1997, at the Cow Palace for the highly coveted belts. The Giant would have the honors of getting the winning pin for his team, as his monstrous body completely covered Hall's minuscule frame eight minutes and fifty-three seconds into the match.

His second tag reign would start on May 17, 1998, when The Giant teamed with Sting in a tag title match in Worcester, Massachusetts, against The Outsiders. The Slamboree affair was a wild and zany bout that not only saw The Giant and Sting win the title, but also saw Hall turn on his longtime friend and partner Nash. The Giant would again have the honors of getting the winning pin, as he climbed aboard Nash at fourteen minutes and forty-six seconds for the win in The Centrum.

On July 20, 1998, The Giant won his third and final WCW tag belt when he teamed with Scott Hall in a battle against their former tag partners, Sting and Kevin Nash. Even though The Giant didn't get the pin for his team on this night in Salt Lake City, he was still happy as he and his partner got revenge on their former teammates. After Bret Hart lent a helping hand to the tag team by interfering in their match, Hall executed his Outsider's Edge maneuver to perfection on Sting for the victory and the right to be called tag-team champions.

The Giant left the WCW in 1999 when he signed a reported ten-year deal with the World Wrestling Federation. He made his federation debut as The Big Show during a steel cage match between Steve Austin and Vince McMahon in February 1999 at the St. Valentine's Day Massacre. The huge grappler surprised everyone, including "Stone Cold," when he ripped his way through the canvas to come to the aid of his new boss. Unfortunately for McMahon and TBS, their secret plan didn't work, as the strong-as-an-ox wrestler wound up breaking the cage when he launched Austin into one of the sides, allowing the Rattlesnake to escape and get the win.

The Big Show would then join Mr. McMahon's Corporation, thinking this would help him get over quicker with the boss and fans.

Until WrestleMania XV, The Show remained a part of McMahon's clan, but one minor slip changed all that for the big fella. At 'Mania, The Big Show took on Mankind for the right to be a guest referee in the main event. But when the powerful grappler chokeslammed him through two chairs, he was disqualified by the ref and reprimanded for his dastardly actions by Mr. McMahon. Not liking how McMahon was talking to him, The Big Show wound up and socked his boss, thus ending his membership with the Corporation.

He then hooked up with Mick Foley, Ken Shamrock, and Test to form the Union to try and combat the Corporation. The foursome took on and defeated Faarooq, Bradshaw, the Big Boss Man, and Viscera at Over the Edge in 1999. The Big Show then turned to the singles circuit and took on and beat The Big Red Machine, Kane, at the 1999 Fully Loaded Pay-Per-View.

Kane's brother, The Undertaker, then called and asked for the big man's services in a tag-team bout against his sibling and his partner X-Pac. The duo wound up besting their challengers for the tag titles at SummerSlam in Minneapolis on August 22, 1999.

A little over two weeks later, the massive tandem would again win the tag straps as they took on and defeated The Rock and Mankind in Albany, New York, in a "buried alive" match.

The Big Show finally hit the big time in the WWF on November 14, 1999, when he won his first-ever World Wrestling Federation Championship at the Survivor Series in Detroit. While his task wasn't a simple one, as The Big Show, who was substituting for an injured Steve Austin, had to take on and defeat The Rock and Triple H in a three-way match for the illustrious belt, he wasn't going to be beat on that night in Michigan. He wanted to do more than just survive at this series—he wanted to walk out of the ring a champion! And that's just what he did after pinning Triple H following his lethal Showstopper finisher.

The Big Show would successfully defend his strap against the Big Boss Man at Armageddon '99, but would lose it to Triple H on January 3, 2000, in Miami, Florida. He would earn another title shot at WrestleMania 2000 after he defeated The Rock—with a little help from his friend and ally Shane McMahon.

But another championship wasn't in the cards for the big guy. As a matter of fact, a trip to the minors was in store for the veteran warrior. In the summer of 2000, after coming off knee surgery The Big Show let himself go, so management sent him to Ohio Valley Wrestling in Louisville, Kentucky, to get back in shape.

"I think going to Louisville was the best thing to ever happen to me," The Show explained in an interview with *WOW* magazine in August 2001. "I'm not just saying this because I'm a company guy. I swear to god that it's the best thing to ever happen to me because it actually gave me the chance to experience what 90 percent of the guys in our business have to go through."

And judging by how The Show has gone on since his return from Kentucky, it's safe to say that another title run may be just around the corner for this wrestling monster.

Booker T

Booker T not only changed bosses in 2001 when Ted Turner sold the WCW to the WWF, he also changed his image—drastically. No more was he concerned about being a role model for his viewing audience; Booker was now interested in making some noise in his new surroundings.

It's safe to say that the 6-foot-3, 250-pound athlete opened some ears and eyes when he burst onto the WWF scene unannounced at the 2001 King of the Ring, attacking "Stone Cold" Steve Austin during his Triple Threat match against Chris Jericho and Chris Benoit for the federation championship.

The chiseled grappler quietly made his way up the aisles of the Continental Airlines Arena to an area outside the ring where Austin was grabbing a chair to use against his opponents. Without hesita-

tion, Booker T sidewalk-slammed Austin through the Spanish announcer's table. Arena security tried to grab hold of the WCW champion but he somehow managed to escape through the sold-out crowd.

But Booker wasn't going to stop there. He was shooting straight
for the WWF stars. Having already attacked the federation champ,
the on-a-mission wrestler was now after the boss of all bosses, Vince
McMahon, Jr., and what better place to do it than in the home arena
of the WWF, Madison Square Garden, during a RAW taping.

Unaware that he was going to be the next sneak-attack victim,
McMahon started off the night by telling the MSG crowd and viewing
audience that the WCW had no place in the world's most-famous arena
and that interferences like the one that happened the previous night in
New Jersey wouldn't be tolerated, especially from WCWers like Booker
T. McMahon also wondered aloud what the T in Booker's name stood
for, suggesting to the all-ears wrestling public that it could very well
represent "terrible, trash, or maybe even temporarily employed."

Meanwhile, about ten blocks away at the federation's theme
restaurant WWF New York, McMahon's "evil son," Shane, along
with Booker, were gloating about what transpired the night before
and plotting their next move, which was about to take place that
night in the Garden.

In a TV interview, Shane talked about how the WCW was going
to invade and take over the WWF, while Booker went one step further and taunted Austin on the air, challenging him to head uptown
for a match to even the score. When Austin saw and heard the
broadcast, he went berserk, telling Vince that the WWF champ
shouldn't be treated in such a manner. His boss suggested that
"Stone Cold" go over to the Times Square location with Kurt Angle
and teach his son and Booker a lesson.

But when the two WWF stars arrived at WWF NY they were informed by a security guard that Booker and Shane had already left.

Back at MSG, Vince was in the middle of the ring bragging to the crowd that Austin and Angle were on their way to the Broadway WWF stomping grounds to open up a can of whoop ass on Booker and Shane, when all of a sudden Shane's entrance music started echoing throughout the Garden, leaving the elder McMahon, for the first time in his life, speechless.

While Shane O'Mac distracted his father, Booker T, the former WCW good guy, snuck up behind the WWF chairman and pummeled him before the New York crowd. Led by the APA (Acolyte Protection Agency), the WWF locker room cleared out in a hurry to help their check-signer, but it was too late as Booker and Shane had already taken care of business and were already out the door.

While this was all so out of character for Booker, who has won over nineteen titles in his career, it got him over real quick with his new crowd, as he was not only acting like a heel, but also attacking some of the top names in the business.

His next WWF interference stop would be in familiar territory, as Booker again came from out of nowhere in Madison Square Garden to nail an unsuspecting Steve Austin. "Stone Cold" was in the middle of pulverizing Tazz and his broadcast partner, Michael Cole, when Booker came up behind him in the ring and gave Austin an up-close and personal look at the WCW championship belt. The now cruel combatant nailed the WWF champ in the face with the strap when he turned around, making World Championship Wrestling the last words Austin saw before his bald head hit the canvas. The WWF cavalry again tried to capture T, but he booked out of the squared circle to a backstage area where Shane O'Mac and a WCW limo were waiting to whisk him away.

Austin would finally get his revenge on the WCW champ when Booker defended his WCW crown against Buff Bagwell on a RAW broadcast from Tacoma, Washington, on July 2, 2001. During the match, Booker was taking it to Bagwell when Austin and Angle came to his aid and the three wrestlers then proceeded to pummel Booker. While he was able to retain his crown due to Buff's disqualification from the match because of Austin and Angle's interference, Booker was getting a taste of his own heel medicine, a flavor he was growing accustomed to ever since he entered the WWF scene.

Booker would also break new ground on July 9, 2001, when he wrestled in the first-ever interpromotional match between the WWF and WCW, as he took on former WWF champ and Olympic gold medalist, Kurt Angle. The two tangled in the old WCW stomping grounds, in Atlanta, Georgia, during a RAW event, with T giving the WWFer a good ol' Southern ass whippin' in front of the Georgia crowd. Never mind the illegal WCW title strap to the face—that's allowed now that he's a heel.

The former WCW superstar got his start in the pro wrestling business in 1989 and has never looked back since. He first started out wrestling for former wrestling great, Ivan Putski, as G.I. Bro for an independent promotion in Houston, but eventually made a name for himself on the tag-team circuit with his brother, Stevie Ray, when they formed one of the greatest tag tandems to ever grace a mat, Harlem Heat.

The duo wrestled all over the indie circuit, taking on any taggers who dared get in their way. Before landing in the WCW in 1993, the brothers wrestled as The Ebony Experience in the Global Wrestling Federation, where they won their first championship on July 31, 1992.

While grappling on the WCW circuit, the duo won the tag title an impressive ten times during their time together, with their first title coming on December 8, 1994, against The Patriot and Marcus Bagwell in Atlanta.

But nowadays, Booker likes going at it alone, just like all the "good" heels.

Christian

Although Christian didn't sign on with the World Wrestling Federation until the summer of 1998, he did start preparing for a career in pro wrestling way before that. He first got a taste of pro wrestling by watching the WWF and Stampede wrestling on TV in Canada and by practicing his moves in his backyard with his best friend, who just happened to grow up to become the wrestling character we all know and love as Edge.

When he was old enough, Christian then took it upon himself to enroll in Sully's Gym in Toronto in 1994, where he was trained for the pro ring by Ron Hutchinson for nine months. When his mentor thought he was ready he put him in the ring with Zakk Wylde, a former pupil of Hutchinson who first started training at Sully's in 1990.

The young gun fared well in his first match against Wylde. Even though he didn't win the bout, Christian didn't lose either, as the two warriors battled to a draw. His next step was to team up with his childhood friend and form a tandem on the independent circuit known as High Impact.

After getting some matches under their belts, the dynamic duo went after their first championship in Emile Dupre's Atlantic Grand Prix promotion, where they tangled as the Suicide Blondes. The taggers battled it out with top-notch talent in the federation like The Super Models and went on to win the Streetfight tag title in December 1997. Christian would also parlay his time on the independent circuit into some singles titles.

He won his first title on his own over Glenn Osbourne on July 18, 1998, in Newport, Delaware, for the East Coast Wrestling Association title. Besides the ECWA belt, Christian also at one time or another held onto the PCW Heavyweight title, the World Pro Wrestling Heavyweight title, and the IWA National title.

Then in August 1994 the WWF came calling and Christian answered. The federation signed him to a developmental contract and sent him to train at the Funkin' Dojo with Dory Funk, Jr. He would make his first WWF appearance a memorable one when he interfered in one of Edge's matches against Owen Hart at Copps Coliseum in Hamilton, Ontario, on September 27, 1998, causing his good buddy to lose.

Less than two weeks later, in his in-ring debut, Christian took on Taka Michinoku for the WWF Light-Heavyweight Championship at the 1998 Judgment Day in Rosemont, Illinois, and took home the gold with Edge looking on.

The longtime friends would kiss and make up and join forces with Gangrel, forming the vicious vampire faction The Brood that wreaked havoc on the entire WWF for some time. Christian and

Edge would then leave Gangrel in the dark and form their own union in the federation tag ranks.

The two went on to win seven WWF tag straps, with the first coming on April 2, 2000, at WrestleMania 2000 in a TLC (Tables, Ladders, and Chairs) match against the Hardy Boyz and the Dudley Boyz in Anaheim, California, and their last coming on April 1, 2001, in Houston, Texas, at WrestleMania X7 at the Astrodome in another TLC bout.

On September 3, 2001, on his home soil in Canada, Christian turned heel on his longtime partner, attacking him with a chair after Edge defended his Intercontinental belt against Lance Storm, solidifying the tag breakup. He would then beat his "brother" at Unforgiven 2001 in Pittsburgh, Pennsylvania, on September 23 for the IC strap.

A little over a month later, Christian would win another singles strap, as he took on and defeated Bradshaw for the European title at a SmackDown! on October 30 in Cincinnati, Ohio. With 2001 coming to a close and the new year in sight, the young Canadian grappler was letting the wrestling world know that he was more than just a successful tag-teamer.

Diamond Dallas Page

Diamond Dallas Page is an extraordinary talent who seems to succeed in whatever endeavor he gets himself involved in. He got his first taste of success in the wrestling business when he managed Badd Company (Paul Diamond and Pat Tanaka) past the Midnight Rockers (Shawn Michaels and Marty Jannetty) in the American Wrestling Association and led them to a World Tag Team title in March 1988.

After tasting the fruitful juices of victory on the managing side of the grappling biz in the AWA, DDP turned his focus to the sunny state of Florida, where he not only added wrestlers such as Scott Hall, Johnny Ace, Bam Bam Bigelow, and Dick Slater to his managing stable, but he also tried his luck and skills behind the microphone. The eager talent even had the honor of calling the wrestling action for Florida Championship Wrestling beside the legendary Gordon Solie.

World Championship Wrestling came calling for his services in 1991 and the New Jersey native jumped at the chance to work as a manager for one of the Big Two promotions. Page took on wrestlers such as Jimmy Garvin and Michael Hayes (the Fabulous Freebirds), while also retaining the services of Hall. He would again guide one of his squads to a championship, as the Freebirds won the tag belts on February 4, 1991.

But while he enjoyed the behind-the-scenes jobs of the wrestling world, Page felt he needed to be closer to the action, so he took to the ring in '91 as one half of a tag duo with Hall, who was at this time known as the Diamond Studd. Once Page competed inside the ropes, there was no turning back. In time, he would not only become associated with Vinnie Vegas (Kevin Nash) and Scotty Flamingo (Raven) and later on the WWF, he would also win ten championship titles.

Over the course of his career, Page has garnered three WCW World Heavyweight belts, three WCW World Tag Team championships, two WCW United States straps, one WCW TV title, and is a one-time WWF World Tag Team title holder. Aside from his achievements on the mat, this wrestling monster also has a life away from the arena. He is one of the few wrestlers that has had success on the outside of the ropes, gaining mainstream attention from his appearances on talk shows like *The Tonight Show with Jay Leno* and in movies like *First Daughter* and *Ready to Rumble*.

Page is also heavily involved in helping children. His own struggles with dyslexia and a fear of reading in public led him not only to write his own autobiography, *Positively Page: The Diamond Dallas Page Journey,* but also to reach out and help kids with reading disabilities. He and his wife, Kimberly, started an organization called

Bang It Out for Books, and have teamed up with the Kid's Book Club and Scholastic Books where they donate money from the wrestler's autograph sessions at schools around the country to buy books to help in the fight against dyslexia and illiteracy.

Their championing of the kid's learning cause also afforded them the pleasure of being invited by President Bush to the White House in Washington during April 2001, where DDP was to read *It's Not Easy Being a Bunny* by Marilyn Sadler to the kids on the lawn during the president's Easter egg hunt. When inclement weather prevented them from hanging out on the White House lawn, Page and Kimberly moved the festivities inside, where the two got to sign autographs and help them dye Easter eggs.

The mat superstar is also in the process of writing a second book, *Positive Thoughts for Kids from A to Z with DDP*, which should hit bookstores with a "bang" just like the first one did.

The Dudley Boyz

No two wrestlers on the pro circuit better epitomize Monsters of the Mat more than the wild and wacky Dudley Boyz, D-Von and Bubba Ray. The two masters of disaster first came onto the World Wrestling Federation scene in August 1999 when Vince McMahon wanted to add some hardcore wrestling personalities to his stable, and almost immediately the table-breaking tandem began crushing more than just furniture during their time between the ropes.

Bubba Ray and D-Von came aboard the WWF after a successful four-year stint with Extreme Championship Wrestling, where they took home an unprecedented eight championship belts from their time spent together on the promotion tag ranks. The deadly duo won their first title belt on March 15, 1997, when they knocked off the

Eliminators (Perry Saturn and John Kronus) in an all-out battle for the right to be called ECW champs. After dropping the straps in a re-match bout between the two teams in Philadelphia on April 13, the Dudleys regained hold of the tag throne on June 20 when they again met up with and defeated the Eliminators.

The mischievous miscreants love to put a hurtin' on their oppo-nents no matter who they are facing. For example, before heading over to the WWF in the summer of '99, the treacherous taggers were in a year-long battle with their younger "brother," Spike, who was trying to find the right partner to help him knock off his successful siblings. Spike first took a shot at his brothers' titles at the 1999 Guilty as Charged Pay-Per-View with New Jack in his corner, but the Dudley duo proved to be too powerful for the twosome.

His next unsuccessful try was at Hardcore Heaven '99 when Spike and Balls Mahoney teamed together for a shot at the tag title. But Spike and Mahoney weren't going to give up after only one try at the tag championship—they would again be ring partners on July 18, 1999, at Heat Wave '99 in Dayton, Ohio, where they would knock off D-Von and Bubba Ray for the belts.

The two teams would square off again a few weeks later, despite D-Von and Bubba's inking a contract with the WWF. The title match took place on August 13 in Cleveland, Ohio, where Spike and Balls lost the belts after having only been champs for less than a month.

But tag reign number seven didn't last very long for D-Von and Bubba Ray, as the gold changed hands one night later when Spike and Mahoney showed some "balls" in the ring and outsmarted and outmuscled their tough foes. Twelve days later, before embarking for the WWF for good, D-Von and Bubba left the ECW on a bittersweet note, as they participated in the first federation taping on TNN on

August 26 in Queens, New York, and won their tag titles back from Spike and Mahoney, only to lose the straps to Tommy Dreamer and Raven before the night was over.

The Dudleys (Bubba Ray and D-Von) then took their rough-and-tumble act to the WWF, where they opened up some eyes by pulverizing their opponents with their lethal move, the 3-D, which stands for Dudley Death Drop. They also loved to plow their challengers through wooden tables that they would bring into the ring during a match whether they won or lost. This devious act, which went over really well with the WWF fans who weren't used to seeing this kind of chicanery in their league, became known around the circuit as "getting wood."

And the monstrous mates wouldn't limit their "getting wood" to just the male WWF personalities. D-Von and Bubba thoroughly enjoyed their "woody" adventures with females as well. The torturous twosome put the moves on luscious ladies like Trish Stratus, Tori, and Molly Holly, not to mention the horrific sight of women's Hall of Fame grappler, Mae Young, who is well into her seventies, going through the pine! These ring warriors have chopped down more trees with their merciless maneuver than a band of lumberjacks in an evergreen forest during Christmastime.

But the damaging duet has done more than just kill a couple of trees, they also have taken home some WWF gold during their time on the circuit. D-Von and Bubba Ray won their first of many WWF tag titles on February 27, 2000, when they beat the New Age Outlaws at No Way Out in Hartford, Connecticut. They have also been involved in memorable matches with both the Hardy Boyz and Edge and Christian, with most of the extraordinary bouts, which usually call for a ladder or two, coming in three-way matches between the three tag squads.

Spike has also found his way to the WWF, making his federation debut on March 19, 2001, during a RAW broadcast from Albany, New York, where he quickly made his mark by helping his brothers win a match over Edge and Christian, gaining their third WWF tag title.

While Spike may not be as big and intimidating as his brothers, the 5-foot-8, 150-pound gladiator knows how to get it done in the ring, giving pro wrestlers all over all the more reason not to mess with any of the Dudley clan.

Edge

W hile Edge may be one of the most remarkably talented young guns in the wrestling world today, how he came to be a professional grappler is even more fascinating. Like almost every other boy in Canada, Edge grew up playing the country's most popular sport, ice hockey. The athletically gifted child also played soccer, volleyball, and basketball while attending Orangeville District Secondary School in Orangeville, Ontario, as a teen.

After school, Edge even spent a lot of time on the ice playing pickup hockey games with his uncles, since his mom was a busy single parent, working two jobs to make ends meet. So one would think that the logical path for the youngster to take would be that of the ice sport he loved to play so much, but he shocked himself and the world when, in 1990 at the age of seventeen, he took a chance and entered an essay contest in the *Toronto Star* on "Why I Want To Be a Pro Wrestler" and won.

The contest afforded him the right to train for one year in Toronto at Sully's Gym, a prize estimated to be worth well over $3,000, with skilled wrestling trainers Ron Hutchinson and Sweet Daddy Skiki. While some parents may have balked at a teenager moving out of the house to another city to follow a dream, Edge's mom was behind him 100 percent.

As a matter of fact, on April 1, 1990, she shelled out $150 per ticket, even though she really couldn't afford it, to take her son to the SkyDome in Toronto to see WrestleMania VI because she knew how much her son loved wrestling. She also knew that, besides her brothers and athletics, she had wrestling to thank for helping keep her son on the straight and narrow. As a kid, whenever Edge wasn't at school or playing sports, he could be found glued to the TV watching either the WWF or Stampede wrestling where his favorite stars like Bret Hart, Shawn Michaels, Ricky Steamboat, Owen Hart, "Cowboy" Bob Orton, Ted DiBiase, and Chris Benoit performed.

But as it turned out, Sully's Gym location in Toronto was a double blessing in disguise for Edge, as he was able to not only learn the tricks of the wrestling trade, but he was also able to enroll in Humber College, where he majored in radio broadcasting.

After completing his one-year training session with Hutchinson and Skiki at Sully's, Edge was ready for his first match. He took to the ring in Monarch Park in Toronto, where he wrestled his first bout as a tag teamer with the El Fuego Kid against Joe E. Legend and Zakk Wylde on June 1, 1993.

From there he teamed with his former foe Legend to form a successful tag duo, Sex and Violence. The tandem worked the indie circuits together and won tag belts in the Canadian Wrestling Federation and Midwest Championship Wrestling.

But Edge would find the most success in his career with his next partner, Christian Cage, who also happened to be a longtime friend and graduate of Sully's Gym. The childhood chums first teamed together as High Impact and the Suicide Blondes and grappled in federations like the Atlantic Grand Prix, where they tussled with another duo The Super Models, and Insane Championship Wrestling (ICW), where they won their first tag titles. They eventually would team together years later in the WWF and form one of the most lethal tandems on the circuit.

But first they had to make their way to wrestling's top promotion. For Edge, his big break can be traced back to an indie match he was wrestling in Whitby, Ontario. Although there were only about 150 people in attendance that night, Edge got lucky because one of the audience members just so happened to be Carl DeMarco, who had strong links to the WWF and one of their top stars, Bret Hart.

At the end of the night DeMarco asked Edge to get him a tape and he'd see what he could do for him. A short while later, DeMarco gave him a call back and asked him if he was interested in wrestling in a trial match at a WWF house show in Copps Coliseum in Hamilton, Ontario, against Bob Holly in 1997. After putting on a good showing, DeMarco helped get him signed with the federation, who immediately sent their new talent to train with Dory Funk, Jr., and Tom Pritchard at the Funkin' Dojo so he could learn to wrestle WWF style.

After some intense training and discussions with management on just who his character would be, the WWF brass, who had tossed around names like Riot and Rage, decided on Edge—an angry young man from Toronto who was always in a dark mood. The federation began cutting and airing promos for their new wrestler in the making, and on June 22, 1998, Edge would make his official debut against Jose Estrada, Jr.

He then appeared by Sable's side as her mystery partner at the 1998 SummerSlam at Madison Square Garden in a mixed-gender match, where the guy/gal duo knocked off their opponents, Marc Mero and Jacqueline.

His next wrestling combination would come when he teamed up with his blood brother, Christian, and their goth-ner in crime, Gangrel, to form a ferocious faction known as The Brood. The threesome went around raising hell in the federation until Edge and Christian decided it was time to fly the dark coop and do some damage of their own on the tag circuit.

But before the newly formed WWF duo found golden success in the tag ranks, Edge took home a singles title, courtesy of his win over Jeff Jarrett. The Canadian-born warrior garnered the Intercontinental belt in memorable fashion as he downed Double J in front of numerous family members and friends at the SkyDome in Toronto on June 24, 1999.

He then tacked on more titles with his partner and friend, Christian, on the tag circuit. The tandem won their first belts at WrestleMania 2000 on April 2 at Arrowhead Pond in Anaheim, California, in a ladder match against both the Hardy Boyz and the Dudley Boyz.

From there the wrestlers from Canada would capture numerous straps together in the immensely talented tag division, but no one would have guessed that these close-as-brothers competitors would ever have trouble coexisting—let alone face each other in the ring! But it happened.

In between their tag matches, the two wrestlers would venture out on the singles circuit in pursuit of individual titles to call their own. One of the first places the two almost collided was in the finals at the 2001 King of the Ring tournament in East Rutherford, New Jersey, on June 24. Both wrestlers made it to the semifinals, with Edge taking on Rhyno and Christian battling Kurt Angle. But the

Clash of the Canadians didn't take place as Christian couldn't get by Angle.

Edge not only got by Rhyno, but he also defeated Angle and took home the prestigious KOTR title. Two months later, he also added another trophy to his showcase, as he knocked off Lance Storm for the IC belt in San Jose, California, stirring up some jealousy in his partner, Christian.

The jealousy eventually led to the two battling in the ring for the IC strap the following month on September 23, 2001, in Pittsburgh, Pennsylvania, with Christian walking away the victor. Edge would get revenge and his belt back less than a month later, as he took on Christian at a No Mercy Pay-Per-View event in St. Louis, Missouri, on October 21. A short while later, Christian again walked away a beaten man when Edge successfully defended his crown over him in November in a steel cage match in Manchester, England, at Rebellion '01.

But Edge didn't let personal issues or emotions stop him from having success on the mat. Once he steps through the ropes, he's all business. On November 12, 2001, during a RAW event in Boston, he pinned Kurt Angle to capture the U.S. title, and then six days later at the 2001 Survivor Series in Greensboro, North Carolina, he beat Test in an Intercontinental/U.S. title unification match.

This Canadian monster likes the view from the top, and plans on staying there!

Ric Flair

Everything about Ric Flair has been outrageous since he broke into the professional wrestling business in the early 1970s. From his flamboyant wrestling attire, to his eye-popping harem of ring escorts, to his outlandish arena entrances, the stylin' and pro-filin' grappler has always had the knack to shock everyone whenever he entered the squared circle.

The gaudy grappler did it again on November 19, 2001, when he not only made a surprise appearance on Monday Night RAW, which was being broadcast from his hometown, Charlotte, North Carolina, but he also dropped a loaded bomb on the wrestling world—he revealed that he was back in the WWF after almost a decade of being away from the federation.

While the Charlotte Coliseum crowd watched and listened to the legendary grappler in amazement that memorable night, no one person was more shocked and numbed by the news than the WWF head honcho, Vince McMahon, Jr. The sole owner of the WWF—at least he thought at the time he was in complete control of the federation— stood in the middle of the ring alongside Kurt Angle with his mouth wide open and his chin almost touching the canvas, as Flair explained how he came to be McMahon's partner in crime.

It turns out that Flair purchased every WWF stock "dumped" by Shane and Stephanie McMahon when the duo decided to form the WCW/ECW Alliance to try and battle their dad for the top spot in the wrestling business, allowing the "Nature Boy" to become a top shareholder in the prestigious wrestling organization. To make matters worse, Flair even shared a beer with McMahon's bitter enemy, Steve Austin, that night after "Stone Cold" pummeled the WWF leader in front of the sold-out crowd, proving that he still had the "flair" for the dramatic.

While Flair came into the WWF on the corporate side of the ropes in late 2001, don't expect him to stay there. Through his thirty years on the mat, Flair has been known to take on any new challenges or challengers that came or got in his way. And just days after his triumphant return to the WWF, the fifty-three-year-old warrior expressed interest in tangling with young lions like The Rock and Steve Austin, and wouldn't rule out tussling with his now WWF partner, Vince McMahon.

The blond bomber came into the pro wrestling world on December 10, 1972, when he took on George Gadaski in Rice Lake, Wisconsin, in an American Wrestling Association (AWA) bout and immediately turned some heads when he wrestled his first-ever opponent to a draw. The reason this was so impressive was that the young wrestling wanna-be was still training under Verne Gagne alongside The Iron Sheik and Ken Patera, and still had a lot to learn about the business, but still managed to somehow come away from the match with a draw.

His next break in the pro ranks came when he crossed over from the AWA to the Mid-Atlantic's National Wrestling Alliance (NWA). He signed on with the association as the tag-team partner of Rip Hawk, and the tandem would win the title belts on July 4, 1974, from Paul Jones and Bob Bruggers after being together for less than a year.

A little over twelve months later Bruggers and Flair would again bump heads, but this time they would not be in a ring and much more was on the line for the two men than just a wrestling title. On October 4, 1975, both men were involved in a plane crash with a band of fellow grapplers that included David Crockett, Tim Woods, and Johnny Valentine and very nearly lost their lives.

While Flair escaped the wreck with a broken back and would return to the squared circle a short while later, Bruggers and Valentine weren't so lucky, as they sustained injuries that were so bad they had to hang up their wrestling boots. But the "Nature Boy" was back on the canvas seven months later as he took on Wahoo McDaniel and scored an impressive win over his talented foe on May 24, 1976, recording his first-ever singles strap in the process. The comeback win not only secured Flair the NWA Mid-Atlantic Heavyweight title that night, but it also started a bitter feud between him and McDaniel.

Over the course of his three-decade career, the "Nature Boy" has feuded with anybody and everybody that has come down the pro wrestling pike. Besides McDaniel, Flair has locked horns with tight-wearers such as Ricky Steamboat, "Rowdy" Roddy Piper, Bobo Brazil, Sting, Lex Luger, Hulk Hogan, Harley Race, Bret Hart, Dusty Rhodes, the Garvin brothers (Jimmy and Ronnie), Randy "Macho Man" Savage, and even the 1950s ring legend Buddy Rogers, the original "Nature Boy," who Flair battled for the right to use the moniker.

But Flair was not only about kicking ass and taking names. He has also been a trendsetter in the rough-and-tough ringed industry. For instance, sixteen months before there was ever a WrestleMania, Flair took part in an NWA wrestling event called Starrcade, which not only drew over 15,000 wrestling fans to the live show, but the Greensboro, North Carolina–held showcase also was seen by over 30,000 viewers on closed-circuit TV throughout the Mid-Atlantic region.

Flair was also well ahead of his time when he formed one of wrestling's first-ever cliques in the Four Horsemen. The wrestling visionary formed his first posse in May 1986 with the Anderson brothers, Ole and Arn, and Tully Blanchard. Over the years, the famous group has had wrestlers like Lex Luger, Chris Benoit, Sting, Barry Windham, Sid Vicious, and Steve McMichael joining the faction, which paved the way for modern-day gangs such as the nWo, The Brood, and DX.

He made his first go-around with the WWF in 1991 when he came on board and tangled with Jim Powers on Canadian soil in Cornwall, Ontario, on September 10 and forced his first federation foe to give in to his lethal figure-four leglock. But Flair wasn't going to stop there. After spending seventeen-plus years with the NWA and WCW garnering countless wins and titles, the cocky grappler made it known to all his new coworkers that he was wrestling's real champion and was willing to prove it to anyone who doubted his word. These words led to numerous battles and feuds during his time in the federation, especially against Randy Savage, Hulk Hogan, and Bret Hart.

Flair proved his worth to the WWF audience on January 19, 1992, in Albany, New York, when the forty-two-year-old eliminated

Sid Justice to win the World Heavyweight title at the thirty-man Royal Rumble tournament. He would win another title strap on September 1, 1992, only to lose it a little over a month later to his nemesis Bret Hart.

When all is said and done, Ric Flair is one wrestling monster who has been around the block a few times, and he keeps coming back.

Mick Foley

E ven though Mick Foley says he's retired from wrestling, don't ever count him out. Despite having a successful career as an author, penning bestselling books such as *Have a Nice Day*, as long as there's blood in his veins and a working federation, the Long Island native will somehow always be involved in the grappling industry.

One of the all-time great Monsters of the Mat, Foley supposedly stepped away from the squared circle for good following a "retirement match" against Triple H at a No Way Out event in Hartford, Connecticut, on February 27, 2000. But he resurfaced less than two months later on April 2 in sunny California, as Linda McMahon coaxed him out of his easy chair to wrestle "one last time" in the main event at WrestleMania 2000 in a four-way dance between him, The Big Show, Triple H, and The Rock for the WWF title.

As soon as this bout was booked, wrestling fans all over thought that Foley, who has eight concussions and over three hundred body stitches to his credit, according to *Have a Nice Day*, was going to headline 'Mania in order to be able to limp into the sunset on top of the wrestling world. But it wasn't in the cards.

Foley would get his licks in on each of the WWF's top stars that night in Anaheim, but he couldn't close out the deal. He would nail The Big Show with a chair, put the Mandible Claw on The Rock, which almost eliminated "The People's Champ," and brawled one-on-one with his nemesis, Triple H. This was his biggest mistake of the night, as Helmsley would again get the best of Foley. After the two foes teamed up to beat on The Rock, Triple H then turned on Foley and nailed him with a leg drop, followed by a Pedigree.

When Triple H couldn't get the three count on his opponent, he turned to a chair for some help and nailed Foley right smack in the noggin with it. He then proceeded to hit him with another Pedigree, which caused Foley to be counted out of the match, leaving Triple H to battle The Rock for the belt. As Foley staggered out of the ring "one last time," the fans gave him a standing ovation to let him know that they appreciated his efforts "one last time."

Or was it?

Just when it seemed like Foley was gone for good, he reentered the ring and nailed Triple H with a barbed wire–covered piece of lumber, almost helping The Rock get the pin and win. But Triple H would have enough left in the tank to avoid the count out, causing Foley to make his "final" WWF exit. Finally?

A little over two months later, Foley's phone would ring again and of course it was a McMahon on the line. No, it wasn't Linda. This time Vince would be calling Mick, asking him to come back to the WWF, but not to wrestle, but rather to turn Corporate.

No. No. He wasn't going to revive the Corporate Ministry or anything like that. He wanted Foley to come on board as the WWF commissioner and the three-time WWF champ accepted. He made his debut as the Commish on July 26, 2000, on a RAW broadcast, adding another title to his wrestling resume.

He loved his new position in the federation, as it not only allowed him to earn another paycheck in the wrestling biz, it also allowed him to be involved in story lines without having to shed anymore blood for cheers. It not only gave him the power to book matches that his loyal fans wanted to see, but it also allowed him to get revenge on some foes who had wronged him in the past.

But this all came to a screeching halt one night in December 2000 when Vince decided, along with his daughter, Stephanie, it was time to put Foley's career to bed "for good," and uttered the words "You're fired!" to his longtime loyal employee.

But four months later Mick's phone rang yet again (you would think he would've gotten caller ID by now?!!?) with Linda again calling on Foley for assistance. No, she didn't want him back as the WWF commissioner. No, she didn't want him to wrestle again for her, but she did want his services in the ring, asking Foley to be a special guest referee at WrestleMania X7 in a Streetfight match between her husband, Vince, and her beloved son, Shane.

Foley of course accepted the offer and once again used the power of his position to extract some revenge on a foe. During the family squabble, Foley had a chance to lay the smackdown on Vince while the WWF owner was yelling at his wife and was about to finish off his son.

After turning in his black-and-white striped ref shirt, Foley supposedly walked out of the ring for "the last time," but after a ten-month layoff, the Foley phone rang—you guessed it—again, on

October 11, 2001. The wrestling great reappeared that night on the WWF scene on an episode of SmackDown! to replace William Regal, who was now running the Alliance as the WWF commissioner.

But a little over a month later, Foley resigned from his post on a November 19, 2001, episode of RAW from North Carolina, where Vince's last words to Mick were appropriately "Have a nice day."

Was this the last chapter to another great Foley wrestling story? Stay tuned to find out.

The Hardy Boyz

The Hardy Boyz, Jeff and Matt, are living proof that if you want something bad enough, you can make your dreams come true no matter how big or small a city you grow up in. The talented wrestling duo grew up in a quaint town in North Carolina known as Cameron, which lies about fifty miles south of Raleigh-Durham, where they practiced their wrestling craft together from an early age.

Even though they've made it to the big time and can live anywhere in the world they desire, the brothers choose to still call Cameron their home, as it's the only place in the world they feel they can be themselves. Matt and Jeff also love to give back to their community whenever they're in town and time allows.

When home, the tag team can often be found visiting their childhood elementary school, Cameron Elementary, where they dreamed as kids to one day wrestle in front of the students and faculty of their high school, Union Pines, where they not only excelled in the classroom but also on the football field. Matt was the straight-A student who liked to play positions like tight end and guard on the offensive side of the ball, while Jeff was the creative student who liked to write and draw and play defense from his linebacker post for UP.

When they weren't engrossed in their studies or athletics, the two could be found at home helping out their dad, Gilbert, on his tobacco farm. While they don't remember their times in the field as fun in the sun, they wouldn't change a thing because they feel that hard work made them who they are today. Growing up, the Hardys also wanted to help their dad, who had lost his wife to cancer when the boys were just nine and twelve years old.

Even at that young an age, the boys knew that losing their mom was going to change their everyday lives drastically and that they had to do whatever was necessary to help their dad carry on.

"[Our dad] was just a real strong man who'd lost his wife and raised two kids," Matt explained in an interview in the September 2000 issue of *Raw Magazine*. "Although he wasn't the wealthiest guy, he always took really good care of us. He was a great guy who always worked hard all his life and always made sure that Jeff and I came first."

Gilbert Hardy, who has also spent over twenty years working for the U.S. Postal Service, is another reason the boys don't mind going home. While Jeff has recently moved into his own place in Cameron, Matt still lives with his dad, loving the opportunity to share his stories from the road and pick his father's brain on a daily basis.

But when they weren't sweating in the tobacco field, Matt and Jeff were still perspiring in their backyard, wrestling with their friends in a makeshift ring made out of old green garden hoses tied to sawed-off wooden chair legs. Their obsession with the grappling game came when Matt and Jeff were fourteen and eleven respectively.

The two siblings became hooked right around the time of WrestleMania IV, when "Macho Man" Randy Savage defeated Ted DiBiase for his first WWF World Heavyweight Championship in Atlantic City, New Jersey. From that moment on the boys were enamored with the entire glitz, glamour, and athleticism that the federation had to offer and together they vowed to one day make it to the WWF, even if it meant wrestling in just one match.

They began not only training and acting the part in their yard with their childhood friends, but they also started saving their money so they could rent a video camera to record their matches and critique and tweak them later. Over the next couple of years, the determined Hardys were not only taping and perfecting their in-ring performances, they were also making their own costumes so they could look the part as well.

The older Hardy, Matt, took the needle and thread in his own hands and not only learned how to sew ring attire, but also how to weave himself and his brother into the world of professional wrestling. One of the first steps the brothers took was forming their own wrestling promotion OMEGA (the Organization of Modern Extreme Grappling Arts), where they performed locally in fairs, carnivals, backyards—quite frankly, for anyone who was interested in having them as entertainment! The two local boys were able to strut their stuff for the first time in front of a live audience on October 15, 1992.

OMEGA not only allowed them the luxury of honing their craft, it also gave them the opportunity to live out one of their childhood dreams—wrestling at Cameron Elementary in front of the students and faculty. Their next break would come in 1993 when the siblings met Gary Sabough, better known as the Italian Stallion, and George

South, the owners of the Professional Wrestling Federation (PWF), who approached the brothers about coming to work with them in their federation.

While the two had never wrestled for an organized outfit before, let alone in a real ring, the Hardys took advantage of the PWF's offer and started taking bumps in the indie federation. Even though the inexperienced wrestlers were getting their heads handed to them each night on the PWF circuit, the contacts they made, especially Sabough, would prove to be invaluable in helping them achieve their lifelong goals.

In 1994, after being out of action for about sixteen weeks, the elder Hardy received a call from the Italian Stallion, who wanted Matt to go with him and wrestle for the WWF, which was looking for an extra at the time. While Matt accepted the offer almost immediately, he realized when he hung up the receiver that he had mixed emotions about heading to wrestling's top promotion without his brother. He also questioned whether or not he was ready to dance with the big boys, as he was only nineteen and only had a handful of matches under his belt.

As if reading his mind, the Italian Stallion eventually called back and extended the offer to Jeff as well, although he was only sixteen at the time. Even though they were only going in as jobbers on the singles circuit, the WWF lined up the youngsters against some pretty stiff competition in their early matches. In his first WWF match in May 1994 in Youngstown, Ohio, Matt found himself in the same ring with the ever-dangerous Nikolai Volkoff, while his brother, Jeff, had no better luck when mat veteran Razor Ramon entered the ring and proceeded to give him the beating of his life. Matt even had a chance to grapple with Rob Van Dam on a RAW Is War broadcast during the ECW Invasion gimmick.

But eventually the two got used to the poundings and found

themselves returning with Sabough every four to five months whenever the WWF needed a helping hand. The federation also began taking notice of the tandem, as they continually referred to themselves as a unit by their last names anytime they worked the region against wrestlers like the Big Boss Man, Ken Shamrock, the Legion of Doom, and Too Much, who would later on become the popular tag duo Too Cool.

The federation finally inked them to contracts in May 1998 when Bruce Pritchard got them to sign on the dotted line, but it wasn't until an incident occurred on the first SmackDown! in April 1999 that the Hardys would catch a real break. Dok Hendrix (Michael Hayes) was conducting an interview in the ring with the gothic gang known as The Brood (Gangrel, Edge, and Christian) and before the session was over the mean-spirited threesome doused the interviewer with a blood-like substance, enraging Hendrix.

About three weeks later, Hendrix would get his revenge on The Brood when he brought along the Hardy Boyz and instructed them to give the threesome a bloodbath of their own on a Sunday Night Heat cablecast. After the Hardys carried out the devious deed they joined forces with Hendrix, who was now going by his previous ring moniker, Michael Hayes.

With Hayes by their side as their manager, the Hardy Boyz began taking on the entire tag ranks, trying desperately to make a name for themselves, so they could one day challenge for the prestigious WWF Tag Team title. Under Hayes's direction, the duo began terrorizing other tag teams by showing up unannounced and interfering in their matches. While this strategy was pissing off the competition, it was causing the fans and management to take notice of the two young guns from North Carolina.

While no duo was safe from their antics at the time, the Hardys especially loved to toy with the members of The Brood. This would eventually get them over when they interfered in a tag title match between The Brood and the Acolytes, costing the dark warriors the title.

On June 29, 1999, the tag team secured their place in wrestling history when they defeated the overpowering Acolytes to become the youngest WWF Tag Team champions ever at twenty-four and twenty-one respectively. What made the win even sweeter for the twosome was that they were able to grab hold of history and the belts in Fayetteville, North Carolina, which was only thirty minutes outside their hometown, in front of a huge group of friends and family, who were present to cheer them on.

An interesting sidenote to their first-ever WWF tag title win was that Matt was so proud and happy that he and his brother had achieved their childhood dream of winning the belt together, that he wore the belt around his waist for two days straight, showing it off to anybody he came in contact with.

The proud pair have since gone on to win five more championship belts together, which includes one WCW tag title, gathering in a huge following along the way. While they may be one of the youngest tag teams in the business today, don't let that fool you, as these North Carolinians know what to do in and above the squared circle. The Hardy Boyz don't just come to the arena ready to rumble, they come fully prepared to wow the audience with their death-defying moves.

One of the first times the team put their moves on display was on October 17, 1999, at the Gund Arena in Cleveland, Ohio, in a match against Edge and Christian at a No Mercy event. The bout was memorable on so many different levels because not only did the Hardys come away with the $100,000 purse and the right to call Terri Runnels their manager, they also came away with the fans' respect, as they performed their magic from high atop the ropes in their first-ever ladder match.

On September 24, 2000, the two teams would meet again, but this time they would battle it out in a steel cage match for the WWF Tag Team title, with the Hardy Boyz walking away with their second title straps. Several months later the two tandems would again keep the fans on the edge of their seats, as they, along with the table-busting Dudley Boyz, would take part in a Triple Ladder match at WrestleMania.

Although they didn't win the 'Mania bout, they were asked back for an encore three-way tag match again against the Dudleys and Edge and Christian, but this time the match would take place at SummerSlam in the familiar surroundings of their home state, North Carolina. Although the brothers again came up empty that night in Raleigh, the crowd didn't go home disappointed, as the brothers put it all on the line in the action-packed Tables, Ladders, and Chairs match in August 1999.

The duo recently has become a trio, as they have added the fiery redheaded grappler, Lita, to their mix. While some may say that the beautiful wrestler is only a part of their entourage because she is the real-life girlfriend of Matt, they need only to witness Lita's high-flying maneuvers once to know that she fits in perfectly with the acrobatic brothers.

In their short time in the pro ranks, the Hardy Boyz have each proven that they can get it done on the singles circuit as well. The 6-foot-2, 225-pound Matt not only has tag titles to show for his efforts, he also has a WWF Hardcore championship and a European title. In a like manner, Jeff also has won some belts on his own. The 6-foot-1, 215-pound gladiator has registered two Hardcore straps, one Intercontinental title, and one WWF Light-Heavyweight title so far in his young career.

Chris Jericho

One way to judge how far a modern-day wrestler has come in his career is to see where he starts and finishes in big event matches involving other federation superstars. And there hasn't been a bigger modern-day bout than The Winner Take All contest at Survivor Series on November 19, 2001, in Greensboro, North Carolina. The main event match pitted Team WWF against Team Alliance, with five megastars from each federation knocking boots to decide the fate of their wrestling organization.

Chris Jericho was not only present in the WWF corner on this memorable night in North Carolina, he also played a significant role in the outcome of the event. The "Millennium Man" got the first pin for Team WWF when he eliminated Shane McMahon from the match after landing his lethal Lionsault maneuver. But the "Ayatollah of Rock 'n Rolla" was not done there.

After The Big Show, Kane, and The Undertaker were abolished, only Jericho and The Rock remained to battle the four leftover Alliance members, Booker T, Rob Van Dam, Steve Austin, and Kurt Angle. The Rock would take out Booker, leaving Y2J to knock off RVD, making the Survivor match now a two-on-two contest.

Just the fact that Jericho was still standing while eight other wrestling stars were backstage watching was a great measuring stick as to where the WWF star had come in his career. The fate of the WWF now rested in the hands of "The People's Champion" and the native of Canada, as they battled "Stone Cold" and Angle.

Angle would be eliminated by The Rock and then Austin would expel Jericho from the match. But before heading backstage, Jericho double-crossed his federation and archrival, The Rock, by knocking the Brahma Bull down, giving "Stone Cold" and Team Alliance a chance at victory.

While this backstab didn't make Jericho the most popular man in the WWF locker room—as a matter of fact, it made him the federation's most wanted man—it did prove that he had come a long way, because no mid-carder would have had the guts to pull such a stunt with the future of the company at stake.

The Rock was able to prevail over Austin and get the win for the WWF over Team Alliance thanks to another federation double-cross when Angle nailed Austin with a championship belt. The next night on RAW Jericho not only had to apologize to Vince McMahon for letting his big ego get the best of him during The Winner Take All bout at the Survivor Series, but he also had to face The Big Red Machine, Kane, one-on-one as per the orders of the federation boss.

While McMahon thought that having Jericho facing the seven-foot mammoth of a wrestler would bring Y2J's ego back down to earth, he was wrong. Immediately following his scolding from the WWF boss, Jericho went out and interfered in The Rock's match against Kurt Angle and then put "The People's Champion" in the Walls of Jericho, making him beg for mercy.

Later on Jericho squared off against Kane, and early on it looked like Mr. McMahon's plan to have The Big Red Machine overpower and punish the athletic Jericho was going to work. But then Y2J landed a Lionsault on his foe and then exited the squared circle to go get some help. His assistance came in the form of a steel chair from ringside, but Kane dispelled that threat when he kicked the weapon out of Jericho's hand.

Kane then slammed his opponent to the canvas and climbed the top rope, looking to take out his challenger, but again Jericho's athletic skills prevailed when, all in one motion, he moved out of harm's way, grabbed the chair, and smacked his flying foe in the noggin, causing him to be disqualified. Then for good measure, the Y2J monster applied the Walls of Jericho and a submission move to Kane before making his way backstage.

Jericho not only left Charlotte, North Carolina, that night with his colossal ego intact, he also kept his feud with the WWF's top dog, The Rock, going at full speed despite McMahon's efforts to tame his out-of-control young gun.

The bad blood between Jericho and The Rock dates as far back as August 9, 1999, which just so happens to be the night The Lionheart made his WWF debut in Illinois. The former WCWer made an outrageous federation entrance when he burst onto the scene unannounced during one of The Rock's interviews.

The federation superstar almost blew a gasket when the new kid on the block not only cut him off on national TV, but he also mocked "The People's Champ" 's mic skills to the viewing audience. Jericho, who debuted in rock star–like fashion with loud music and py-rotechnics, let his new fans know that he was not only there to be the WWF's new party host and savior, but also to save them from boring wrestlers like The Rock who have no verbal mic skills.

While these bold statements made both of the People's Eyebrows rise, it was only a taste of what was to come that night and in the near future from the WWF rookie. From the get-go, Jericho wanted to send a message to the WWF's number one star that he wasn't afraid to challenge him for the top slot in the federation.

The young lion put his words into action on his first night on the job when he pissed off The Rock and the WWF's *biggest* star, The Big Show, who stands in at 7-foot-2 and tips the scales at 500 pounds. Jericho again brought the Chicago RAW crowd to their feet when he reentered the Allstate Arena and not only heckled "The People's Champ" and The Big Show, but also interfered in their match.

Y2J would continue his enticing ways for the next few months, as he sprung sneak attacks on federation stars like Ken Shamrock, the Road Dogg, and The Undertaker. But on December 12, 1999, Jericho put his antics on hold and went after WWF gold. He won his first federation title when he beat Chyna for the Intercontinental strap down in the sunny state of Florida.

The two would clash again on January 3, 2000, for the IC belt in Miami, and when all was said and done they had to share the title due to a controversy that occurred during the match, as two refs wound up being involved in the match's outcome. One referee claimed that Chyna's shoulders were pinned to the mat and awarded Jericho the win, while the other zebra counted Jericho out and claimed Chyna to be the victor. Since wrestling refs don't have the luxury of video replay to help them make the correct call as in other sports, the federation decided it best to name the two wrestlers co-holders of the title.

Later on that month, Jericho would take sole possession of the IC belt when he again went up against Chyna, but this time Hardcore Holly was in the mix too. The three stars grappled in a Triple Threat match at Royal Rumble 2000, with Y2J besting Holly by locking him in his lethal Walls of Jericho move for the win.

Two months later in California, Jericho would add another belt to his resume, when he took on Chris Benoit and Kurt Angle on wrestling's biggest stage, WrestleMania. The three men battled in a unique match that put two belts, the Intercontinental and the European, on the line where the first wrestler to pin someone would garner the IC belt and the second man to score a three count would earn the right to be called Euro champ.

Benoit defeated Y2J in the opening bout for the IC strap, but the "Millennium Man" did not go home empty-handed, as he scored a pin and win over Angle that night in Anaheim, becoming the new European champion.

Now that he had some gold behind him, Jericho again went back to torturing top WWF stars. His next victim(s) was none other than the head honcho Vince McMahon's daughter, Stephanie, who also happened to be "married" to Triple H.

Y2J harassed Stephanie not only because she was an easy target, but also because she was "the wife" of the heavyweight champ at the time. The sly grappler figured if he insulted her enough he would entice Triple H to put his belt on the line in order to try and stop Jericho's verbal abuse of his "spouse."

On April 17, 2000, Jericho's plan worked to perfection . . . well, almost. He got his chance to battle Triple H for the WWF championship and won, but his belt was retracted shortly afterward as the original referee of the match was knocked out, causing another striped-shirt-wearing official to enter the ring and call the match.

After Jericho pinned his foe and garnered his first-ever WWF championship, Stephanie, her brother, Shane, and Triple H would protest the match's outcome. The trio cited that the win and title change was invalid because the original ref was not present to make the call, forcing the replacement referee to reverse his decision.

Even though Jericho was upset by the call change, he had sent a message to the McMahon/Helmsley regime that the "Ayatollah of Rock 'n Rolla" was for real and could one day beat Triple H in a match whether it was for a belt or not.

Strangely enough Stephanie began taunting Y2J at his matches claiming that she wanted to make his life hell. But Y2J saw it differently, as did Triple H! Jericho believed that the WWF champion's "wife" secretly had a crush on him and kept showing up at his matches because she couldn't get enough of him. Whether this was true or not was anybody's guess at the time, but one thing that was for certain was that Triple H wasn't happy about his "wife's" actions or Jericho's remarks.

While these accusations baffled Stephanie, she became even more surprised and disgusted when Jericho planted a wet one on her lips during a WWF TV taping. This really sent Triple H over the edge and he now wanted revenge on the "Millennium Man" in the worst way.

So one night, Triple H, his "wife," and a couple federation friends tried to goad the pesky Jericho out to the ring so they could give him a surprise pummeling. The evildoers had Steph confront Jericho and ask him to meet her in the ring so she could get some more lip service. But Y2J was one step ahead of his sneaky attacker and wasn't buying what she was selling. Even though he considered himself a good kisser, he knew Stephanie didn't want him between the ropes so she could get some more lovin'. He smelled a rat from where he was and opted to address the situation later from the giant Titan Tron screen above the ring entranceway.

When their plan seemed to fail, Triple H and one of his longtime friends, X-Pac, pretended to get into an argument and decided to settle their differences in the ring. Thinking he had outsmarted Stephanie and her entourage, Jericho decided to watch the match from ringside; a move he would regret when it was too late.

Y2J would get ambushed by Triple H, X-Pac, and the Road Dogg, leaving the "Millennium Man" begging for mercy, especially after taking several sledgehammer shots to the chest from Triple H. When Jericho recovered from his nasty beating, he was up to his old tricks, making Triple H's life a living hell by interrupting his matches and again by insulting his "wife."

In July 2000, the two superstars would duke it out in a bloody bout at Fully Loaded in a Last Man Standing match, where the winner would be determined after one of the combatants couldn't continue. And just when it looked as though there wouldn't be a declared winner in the long, drawn-out war, as both participants were out cold after smashing through the announcer's table, Triple H rose to his feet long enough to grab the win.

While Jericho once again didn't come out on top against Triple H, he again opened some eyes around the WWF circuit showing that he could brawl with the best of 'em. He would soon learn that he had lots of wrestlers who wanted to knock the talented trash-talker off his perch. Monsters of the mat like Kane, William Regal, Chris Benoit, Kurt Angle, and The Rock would all come knockin' on the door of the son of former New York Ranger hockey great Ted Irvine. And being the good party host that he is, Jericho would always be there to answer the bell.

Kane

In the modern-day world of professional wrestling no grappler greater exemplifies the monster of the mat mold better than The Undertaker's younger brother, Kane.

Ever since his emergence on the World Wrestling Federation scene in the 1997 Hell in a Cell match between The Undertaker and "The Heartbreak Kid" Shawn Michaels, the gruesome gladiator has made a lucrative living by terrorizing the other federation superstars.

Standing in at seven feet tall, with a 326-pound muscle-ripped frame, Kane's looks alone can kill an opponent's desire before a match even begins. The brutal brawler enters the arena each night to haunting music, followed by streaks of fire blazing from each of the ring posts upon his cue when he gets to the squared circle.

But the intimidation doesn't stop there.

Once he's between the ropes, his look is even more frightening up close to his foes. They stare across at a devil of a being who is clothed in a bloodred outfit, accompanied by a face-covering mask, making them wonder aloud, "What the hell have I gotten myself into?"

From the beginning of his career, a mask always seemed to follow Kane around, but the big difference was that he wasn't always this frightening or successful. He began working the independent circuits in the early 1990s for federations in and around the States and the world. His desire to make a name for himself in the pro wrestling world gave him the opportunity to travel and see places like Japan, the Dominican Republic, Puerto Rico, Florida, and Tennessee.

One of his first stops was in Memphis, where he signed on with Jerry "The King" Lawler's United States Wrestling Association. "The King" immediately put the monster of a man to work as a masked warrior called the Christmas Creature. When the holiday brute didn't pan out, he tossed the facial cover aside and began working the ropes as Doomsday.

The WWF would come calling in 1993 courtesy of Lawler and his working relationship with the federation. The USWA head honcho, who worked in both organizations at the time, brought his employee along as one of his masked henchmen, whom "The King" wanted to use to knock off Bret "The Hitman" Hart.

Not only did he jump at the chance to take part in a story line in the WWF, the concealed assassin also parlayed this opportunity into another freelance job in the top federation when he hooked up with Shawn Michaels and wrestled as one of his Knights in a match at the 1993 Survivor Series. "The Heartbreak Kid" had three Knights, The Black Knight (Kane), The Blue Knight (Greg Valentine), and The Red Knight (Barry Horowitz), in a match that evening in Boston against the Hart Brothers, Owen, Bret, Bruce, and Keith.

Kane would then briefly return to the USWA, but moved on

when Jim Cornette recruited him in August 1995 to wrestle for his promotion, Smoky Mountain Wrestling. During his time in SMW he not only found success as the Unibomb, but he also struck gold in more ways than one.

On April 7, 1995, the Unibomb, along with his partner Al Snow, defeated the Rock 'n' Roll Express at Blue Grass Brawl III in Pikeville, Kentucky, for the right to be called tag team champions. He also found the love of his life, Maurisa, who would eventually become his wife.

Later in that year, Lawler and the WWF again came calling with another gimmick for the wrestler to play—Issac Yankem. Yankem came on board as Lawler's personal dentist when "The King" claimed his choppers were ruined during a "Kiss My Foot" bout with Bret "The Hitman" Hart. Yankem must have had all of his own wisdom teeth yanked out before he agreed to take on this persona because it was not a smart move at all. As a matter of fact, it was probably more painful to watch this character than an actual trip to the dentist!

His next stop on Bad Gimmick Road was in 1996 when the WWF decided it would be a good idea to bring in fake versions of Diesel and Razor Ramon, who had just left the federation for the greener pastures of the WCW. The former evil tooth puller was chosen to play the fake Diesel while Rick Bogner was picked to play the fake Ramon. The two competed together in a match at the 1996 Survivor Series, but would only last on the circuit for a few months after that.

He then packed up and headed back to Tennessee and the USWA for the summer of '97, where again he took on his Doomsday persona. This would be a good move as D-day garnered a heavyweight championship on July 13, 1997, in Nashville against Spellbinder. He dropped the belt in a rematch against his formidable foe less than two months later on September 6 in Memphis. But that didn't matter, as the WWF was again calling, and this time it was going to be for keeps.

On October 5, 1997, The Big Red Machine made his official WWF debut as Kane, the younger brother of The Undertaker, during the main event of the In Your House "Bad Blood" event in St. Louis, Missouri. The memorable night would not only mark the coming-out party of the mat monster, it would also introduce the WWF fans to the first-ever "Hell in a Cell" match. On this dreadful evening, The Undertaker and the self-proclaimed Showstopper, Shawn Michaels, would go one-on-one in a steel cage that surrounded the ring and battle it out for the right go to the Survivor Series for a shot at Bret Hart and the WWF Championship.

'Taker would beat Michaels to a bloody pulp in the inaugural Cell match and just when it looked like he was going to finish off his fallen foe, the lights went out momentarily and out of the dark emerged Paul Bearer accompanied by an unknown beast of a wrestler, who turned out to be Kane.

The grotesque grappler then proceeded to rip off the door of the cage and enter the ring with the two stunned wrestlers. He approached his long-lost brother, who was puzzled by his presence, as he thought his younger brother was dead, and nailed him with a Tombstone Piledriver before The Undertaker could even react. Kane then left the ring with Bearer, and Michaels covered the down-and-out 'Taker for the win and chance at the heavyweight title.

This was just the start of the family feud between the two Brothers of Destruction. In his early years in the federation, Kane's main focus was not on title belts or championships, it was to get revenge on his older brother, who supposedly "killed" their entire family by setting their home ablaze when they were younger. But The Undertaker wanted no part of a sibling squabble, claiming that he would not square off against his own flesh and blood.

Kane would create havoc whenever he entered an arena during a WWF event. The ferocious freak would interfere in matches just for the hell of it, especially ones that his relative was wrestling in. But The Undertaker would not concede to a match against his brother—until after the 1998 Royal Rumble, that is!

Kane would push his brother over the edge after what he did to The 'Taker at the main event match in San Jose, California. The Undertaker was scheduled to take on Shawn Michaels one-on-one in a casket bout at The Rumble, but "The Heartbreak Kid" had other plans. All during the match, grapplers would come from backstage to try and help Michaels beat his adversary and when the ring became cluttered with wrestlers pounding on The Undertaker, Kane emerged from behind the curtain to help out his outnumbered brother.

After the overpowering wrestler cleared the cage of all the rats, the entire wrestling world thought the two were going to kiss and make up. But Kane had other thoughts—evil ones, of course! He took full advantage of being alone in the ring with The Undertaker and not only pummeled him to death but also stuffed him in the casket, with the help of Paul Bearer, who was now also on the scene. Adding insult to injury, Kane also doused the coffin with gasoline and set it ablaze.

After supposedly sending The 'Taker to his maker there may have been a hint of a smile behind that mask, but a short while later Kane wasn't smiling, as his brother miraculously reappeared on a RAW broadcast, setting the stage for a hellacious brothers battle at WrestleMania XIV. The elder sibling got his revenge on Kane in 'Mania in Boston, but it wasn't easy, as The Undertaker had to land three successive Tombstone Piledrivers in order to get the three count.

The two would cross paths several more times, but Kane no

longer wanted to wrap his hands around his brother's neck. He now wanted to get his hands on some federation titles and what better title to go after than the WWF World Heavyweight Championship?

Kane took on "Stone Cold" Steve Austin at the 1998 King of the Ring event in Pittsburgh, Pennsylvania, in a First Blood match, where the first wrestler to bleed would be declared the loser. With a little help from his brother, The Undertaker, Kane won his first WWF championship when Austin bled first.

Since then the monster of the mat has garnered several different championship titles and has drawn more blood than a vampire on Halloween night. One of his most recent and impressive title wins came on May 21, 2001, at Judgment Day 2001 in Sacramento, California. The big red monster knocked off Triple H in a barbarous chain match to take home the Intercontinental Championship.

Lita

The WWF is not only filled with super male grapplers. The world's top wrestling federation has its share of female stars who bring the crowds to their feet, and one of these sexy sirens is Lita.

But unlike the other top-notch performers, this fiery redhead had no idea when she was growing up that one day she would become a professional wrestler. As a matter of fact she didn't have much time to dream or think about anything in her future as she led a nomadic childhood, moving around the country four times before she was twelve years old.

Lita would soon learn that her frequent traveling as a child would pay off for her later on in her life, especially in the world of professional wrestling where she is on the road for over 200 shows per year. The young lady, who was born in Ft. Lauderdale, Florida, learned from an early age how to adapt quickly to new surroundings and also how to live life spontaneously.

After graduating from high school a year early at the age of seventeen, Lita picked up and moved out on her own to Atlanta. She stayed in Georgia for six years, the longest she's ever lived anywhere in her life, but soon got the itch to pack up again and find a new place to live that offered her some new challenges.

Through one of her friends, the fly-by-the-seat-of-her-pants gal did find a new home in Washington, D.C., which was certainly going to be a challenge because, according to an article in the December 4, 2001, edition of *WWF's Extreme Magazine*, Lita was not only going to be living in a house that doubled as a recording studio and tattoo parlor with seven guys, but she was also going to be spending her nights sleeping in the laundry room.

During her time in Washington, Lita became interested in music and took up playing the bass guitar. This would also benefit her later on in her mat career, as her musical talents allowed her the chance play in, work for, and travel with several bands, again getting her used to living life out of a suitcase.

While she enjoyed playing with bands such as 3 Card Trick, Lita knew that her future didn't lie in music. She loved going from place to place, meeting, greeting, and performing for different people every night and feeling the huge rush of the audience, but there was something missing from the music industry that didn't make her pursue it further. So again, the adventurous girl packed up and moved on, this time finding herself in Europe.

After exploring Europe for a month, Lita moved back to the States to Richmond, Virginia, where she had a couple of friends and more importantly, where the rent was cheap enough for her to continue to try and find her calling in life.

It wouldn't take very long after her return to the United States for Lita to stumble upon her passion. One night in the summer of 1997, her friends were watching a wrestling program on TV, which the well-traveled girl first dismissed as being stupid—until her eyes caught hold of the Luchadore wrestlers from Mexico.

The high-flying performers impressed her so much that she knew she wanted to try it out for herself, even though she didn't know a thing about the wrestling industry. Her first step was to take judo lessons so she could learn how to protect herself and also so she could polish up on her athletic skills, which she really hadn't used since high school, where she was a member of the swimming team.

Also during this time, Lita saved up her money so she could fly down to Mexico to learn from the experts themselves. By 1998 she was ready to head south on her own and give Mexican wrestling a whirl, even though she didn't know anything about where to go or who to see.

But her determination and desire led her to the right people once she got herself settled in Mexico. Lita, who was relying on the Spanish she learned in high school, found the school where the Lucha Libre was being taught and began showing her face there each night until someone took notice of her.

The persistent American began training with Ricky Santana, Dave Sierra, Kevin Quinn, and Miguel Perez and after six weeks of the hard-knock life, the Mexican grapplers gave her some chances to show what she could do. She began a brief stint with the Empresa Mexicana de Lucha Libre (EMLL), where she performed some small vignettes and also was given a spot as a manager.

But before she could learn all the ins and outs of the Mexican style of wrestling her money ran out, forcing her to return to the States before she really wanted to. Still determined to make a go of a career between the ropes, Lita talked to her newfound friends and trainers before she left Mexico and they agreed to continue to help her learn the tricks of the trade if she ever decided to come back to their homeland.

Keeping that in the back of her mind, Lita returned home and saved up every dime she could so she could one day return to the Spanish-speaking country to follow her wrestling dreams. Once she had enough cash in the kitty, Lita once more packed her bags and headed south of the border to find her mentors.

She would take a three-week crash course in an amateur ring that used garden hoses as the ropes, but that didn't matter to Lita, as she was learning to take bumps from some of the most talented athletes on the Mexican circuit. She would again return to the U.S. after her cash well ran dry.

Lita's next stop was the windy city of Chicago, where she trained twice a day at the Steel Domain for a week before heading out on the independent circuit to see if she had what it took to make a living in the industry.

One of her first stops was the National Wrestling Alliance (NWA), where she ran into two young wrestling hopefuls, the Hardy Boyz, who would become two very important people in her life both on a personal and professional level.

While working the indie circuit in North Carolina, the duo invited Lita to come train with them and several other wrestlers on Sundays, where they all worked on perfecting their moves in hopes of one day being discovered. Once again Lita found herself being the only girl on the block, but she didn't mind nor did she want any special treatment from the boys. Whatever the guys were doing, she wanted to give it a shot no matter how difficult or dangerous it was.

The high-flying times she spent training with the Hardys and wrestling on the indie circuit as Angelica would eventually pay off as she was offered a spot to wrestle on the pro ranks by Paul Heyman of Extreme Championship Wrestling in 1999. But the only drawback to the deal was that the ECW honcho only wanted her to come aboard as a valet, not as a wrestler.

She reluctantly took the job, hoping to one day have the opportunity to show that she could keep up with the big boys. Keeping the Angelica moniker, she got her first Pay-Per-View exposure on ECW's Heat Wave on July 19, 1999, where she joined forces with Danny Doring. A short while later, Doring and his partner, Road Kill, would ask for and receive the managerial services of the new and beautiful ECW babe.

On August 28, 1999, the trio would take on and beat Chris Chetti, Super Nova, and another ECW beauty, Jazz, at ECW Arena. Even though Angelica, who was also known on the circuit as Miss Congeniality, was able to strut her stuff in the ring that night against Jazz, she was not happy about her future in the federation. She wanted more ring action than the ECW was offering.

Noticing her frustration, ECW superstar Rob Van Dam introduced her to Dory Funk, Jr., who invited her to come train at his camp with twenty-three other wrestling hopefuls. She accepted and eventually graduated from the Funkin' Dojo with high marks. She returned to the ECW for a short while and grappled in her final federation PPV, Anarchy Rulz, where she again tussled with Jazz.

In the meantime, Funk, who had helped stars such as Edge, Christian, Kurt Angle, and Test get started, was sending out wrestling tapes of his prized student to the WWF Talent Relations department, hoping to strike up some interest in his talented graduate. The teacher got a tape in the hands of the WWF VP of Talent Relations, Bruce Pritchard, and a short while later the redhead was offered a developmental contract.

She would first wrestle in dark matches for the federation, mostly with a Latino grappler called Essa Rios. One night while tangling with Rios in the ring, she landed one of her impressive moonsaults on her foe, causing not only the audience to "oooh" and "aaah," but also upper management.

Before long, the high-flying wrestler, now known to the wrestling world as Lita, debuted as the official sidekick of Rios, displaying her moonsaults and hurricanranas for all to see when her partner feuded with fellow Latino Eddie Guerrero and his sidekick, Chyna.

Despite being two times smaller than the Ninth Wonder of the World, Lita held her own against Chyna, using her quick reflexes and athletic ability to counter Chyna's power and experience. She even managed to embarrass Chyna one night when she stripped the proud grappler down to her bra and panties at Backlash 2000 in Washington, D.C., after a Rios and Guerrero match.

But her association with Rios was to come to a close a short while later. On May 22, 2000, Rios joined the Godfather in a bout against Dean Malenko and Perry Saturn on an episode of RAW. The Latino wrestler not only got caught battling Malenko and Saturn in the ring that night, he also was seen fraternizing with the Godfather's Hos, causing Lita to blow her stack. She then took matters into her own hands, by interfering in Rios's match, causing him to be pinned by the bald-headed Saturn.

The following night on SmackDown! would be a memorable one as she not only broke free from her ties with Rios, who was blaming his sidekick for his then losing streak, but she also would once again meet up with her good friends, the Hardy Boyz, after one of the brothers (Matt) battled with Rios in the ring.

After Rios lost to Matt Hardy, he dragged Lita into the squared circle and humiliated her in front of the crowd, tossing his partner out of the ring onto the concrete floor. A few minutes later, the Hardys came back out into the arena to rescue their longtime friend.

In the months that followed, Lita became the new manager for the Hardy Boyz. But she also made a name for herself when she took on and defeated Stephanie McMahon-Helmsley on August 22 for the WWF Women's Championship.

Lita now became a fan favorite and hot commodity on the WWF circuit, receiving challenge after challenge from women and men wrestlers alike. To date, Lita has shared the ring with superstars such as Trish Stratus, Jacqueline, Torrie Wilson, Triple H, Edge, Christian, Stacy Kiebler, Chris Benoit, and countless others.

At one point, Dean Malenko challenged the flame-haired beauty to a stipulation match, where if he won, she had to go out with him on a date. After losing the match to Malenko, Lita held true to her word and went on a date with the enamored grappler. Little did he know that the Hardy Boyz would be waiting to pound his head in at the date's conclusion—sending a message to the wrestling world that if you mess with Lita, you also will have to answer to Matt and Jeff Hardy.

The McMahons

While the McMahons are not your typical perfect TV family like the Waltons or the Bradys, it's safe to say that the wrestling clan is the most successful family on the tube today. As a matter of fact, it's a given that sweet little John Boy would've been told to "Shut up!" by Stephanie. Or her brother Shane might have come into the bedroom to open up a can of whoop ass on the soft-spoken farm boy. Marcia and the rest of the Brady kids also wouldn't have survived a second with the McMahons. The oldest Brady girl would've been hit in the face by more than just a football by one of her siblings if she lived in the McMahon household. Who knows, she may have been hit with the same sledgehammer that Stephanie ordered her "husband," Triple H, to use on her dad, Vince, a few years back.

But the one thing the McMahons do have in common with the Waltons and Brady Bunch is that they were all prime-time hit shows. The current WWF product can be seen in more than 130 countries and in nine different languages each week, making the names Vince, Shane, Stephanie, and Linda watercooler and lunchroom material each day around the globe.

While wrestling's first family no longer has a private life, as their dirty laundry gets aired out on TV every Sunday, Monday, and Thursday night, they don't mind as long as they keep on getting close to a billion smiles—and dollars, for that matter—in return for their efforts each year.

And they have no one to thank more than the king of their castle, Vince McMahon, Jr.

In 1982, Vince had the brains and guts to purchase the Capital Wrestling Corporation from his dad, Vince, Sr., and turn it into the lucrative business it is today. The younger McMahon not only wanted to change the product from sports to sports-entertainment, but he also had the vision to market his events on a global level as opposed to the commonplace regional efforts. According to an article in *Newsweek* on February 7, 2000, the idea behind the brand change was to admit to the matches not being real, and to also add ongoing plots and story lines to the bouts, giving the product a soap opera–like feel. Vince's tweakings were also to attract a wider audience that would tune in each week to see what was going to happen to their favorite superstar(s) next in this new wild and wacky world. Just like he had hoped, it took off big time!

Today the WWF attracts over a half billion viewers worldwide each week, while also raking in the big bucks at the box office for their live event performances. To his credit, Vince knows just where to find the talented performers who'll carry out his master plan to perfection each and every night. McMahon not only finds his wrestlers in gyms pumping iron, he also plucks them off the basketball court, the football and baseball fields, the modeling catwalk, the boxing ring, the Olympic stage, and even ice-cold hockey rinks!

After his CWC purchase, Vince, Jr.'s first big step in the right direction came in 1984 when he inked Hulk Hogan to a deal. The shrewd North Carolina native saw something in Hogan that he believed transcended wrestling. He saw someone with the potential to carry his federation on his shoulders to heights it had never seen. The icing on the cake for McMahon was when he saw Hogan in action on the big screen as Thunderlips in the hit movie *Rocky III*. McMahon loved the way Hogan's character jumped off the screen and left a lasting impression on the audience.

The duo combined their efforts, along with the WWF's top heel at the time, "Rowdy" Roddy Piper, and made wrestling the place to be and the event to see in the 1980s. McMahon and co. really found gold when they introduced the world to the ultimate wrestling show, WrestleMania, on March 31, 1985, at the world's most popular venue, Madison Square Garden in New York.

McMahon and Hogan rode the Rock-N-Wrestling wave for close to ten years together in the WWF. Just when it looked as though interest in his stars and federation might be waning in the '90s—especially with Hogan jumping ship to the WCW—McMahon pulled "Stone Cold" Steve Austin out from under a rock and created a whole new sensation in the WWF brand once again. Some wrestling experts were again labeling McMahon a genius, going as far as saying that the "Stone Cold" era was even bigger than the "Hulkamania" era.

There was no stopping Vince, as he introduced the world to grappling greats like The Rock, Triple H, and Chyna, who each brought something new and exciting to the table. Wrestlers from all over the world wanted to be in on McMahon's action and they were willing to do anything to be a part of the federation. British import William Regal once even kissed Mr. McMahon's bum in the center of the ring just to stay employed in the WWF.

Three WWFers who didn't need to do any ass kissing in order to get a job in the WWF were his son, Shane, his daughter, Stephanie, and his wife, Linda. The trio slowly was worked into the mix and wrestling has never been the same since.

Shane was being groomed for a WWF post from an early age. As a kid growing up, he not only helped promote upcoming federation events by handing out flyers and tacking up posters in the surrounding neighborhood, he also would help clean up the arenas after events were over. At the age of nineteen the curious son of the boss was looking to find his niche in the federation, so he tried his hand at several different jobs in the organization. At one time or another Shane could be found wearing the black-and-white striped referee's shirt, holding a ring announcer's microphone, or handling tools to help construct and deconstruct the ring.

In July 1998, he was sitting ringside at the announcer's table with a mic in front of him on Sunday Night Heat, voicing his opinions on the grappling game. But that didn't last very long, as he would be directly involved in the WWF story lines two months later when he would dramatically turn his back on his dad. On October 26, 1998, Shane announced to the wrestling world that he had rehired "Stone Cold" after his father had just dismissed the WWF superstar.

The young millionaire's son explained to the RAW viewing audience and his dad just what he did when he said: "I just wanted to tell you personally that it was me, it was me, Dad, that hired 'Stone Cold' back. It was me. Hey, I guess I finally have your attention. After twenty-eight years, I finally have your attention. I've seen superstars come and I've seen superstars go and why, Dad? Why? Because it's always been about your ego. You said it yourself, 'No one is big-

ger than Vince McMahon.' Oh no! All my life people have asked me, 'Boy, what's it like to be Vince McMahon's son? Wow, wasn't that great?' And I have lied year after year to protect you. To protect our family name. Well, the lying stops now! I'm tired of it! You never cared about me. Everything . . . I couldn't do anything right for you!"

He also stirred the WWF pot in 1999 during a Streetfight match against X-Pac. Shane appeared on the scene alongside two of his real-life best friends, Pete Gas and Rodney, when he tried to get over with the fans as a rich, arrogant, snobby heel. This plot, which couldn't have been pulled off without the awesome work of X-Pac, worked so well that it propelled Shane and his buds to make an appearance at Wrestle-Mania XV. He would also become involved in family squabbles with his sister, Stephanie, and other WWF personalities such as Triple H and Test and would make his parents proud by winning a couple of federation titles—the Hardcore and the European—along the way.

But all of those feuds and accolades piled on top of one another can't even compare to the battles he's had with his father, especially the ones where the two McMahons actually rolled up their sleeves and duked it out in the ring. On April 12, 1999, Shane slapped his dad on an episode of RAW in front of a shocked wrestling audience. But on March 26, 2001, Shane stunned his dad worse than Steve Austin ever did, when he purchased the WCW right out from under his dad's nose, vowing to knock his dad off the top of the wrestling

Howard Kernats

When The Undertaker enters the ring full of his
"American badass" attitude, his opponents should beware—
they are about to be taken for their Last Ride.

J&E Sports Photography

Though Christian and Edge have the right moves to charm the ladies, don't let their smooth exteriors fool you— they've also got the moves to take down their foes.

Howard Kerr

Black Jack Brown

The Billion-Dollar Princess doesn't look happy,
but we all know she always gets her way.

Kane is one of the all-time great monsters of the mat.

"Whazzzup?!?"

If you mess with Steve Austin, you'll be in trouble—
and "that's the bottom line, 'cause Stone Cold said so!"

Howard Kernats

Booker T is gonna unleash a scissors kick
on the next sucka who challenges him.

One thing you can be sure of with Trish
is that "Stratusfaction" is always guaranteed.

mountain. He took his first step at achieving his goal when he took on and defeated his dad in a Streetfight at WrestleMania X7 in Houston, Texas, on April 1, 2001.

Shane would also reveal that he wasn't alone in his "evil plot" to put his dad out of business, as his sister, Steph, who was now the proud new owner of ECW, was also "in on the plan." Together, the two McMahon siblings joined forces and formed the WCW/ECW Alliance, a group of formidable wrestling stars who were glad to climb on board to help squash the elder McMahon.

But Stephanie wasn't always against her dad. In her early federation years, the precious princess was just daddy's little girl, who was first seen on camera on November 30, 1998, during a cablecast, as she bumped into Steve Austin in one of the WWF hallways. Her WWF debut wouldn't come until four months later when she was "kidnapped" by The Undertaker on March 29, 1999.

After the devious deed, Vince and Shane searched and searched until they found Stephanie locked away in the bowels of the Continental Airlines Arena in New Jersey frightened out of her wits. But the WWF's dark warrior and his evil Ministry didn't stop the stalking there, terrorizing Steph whenever the opportunity arose. For some time, the only place the youngest McMahon felt safe was in the arms of her millionaire daddy.

The most serious 'Taker strike came on April 26, 1999, during a RAW broadcast when the Lord of Darkness, who had again abducted Stephanie, tried to take her over to the dark side against her will and make her his bride. The Undertaker and his cronies, who included Paul Bearer performing the ceremonies, informed the wrestling world that they would hear wedding bells tolling on that scary night in Hartford, Connecticut.

Several WWFers tried to stop the monster of the mat from going through with the insane plan, but their efforts were thwarted every time by the Ministry. To everyone's surprise, the only one who was able to get close enough to rescue Vince's tied-up daughter was "Stone Cold" Steve Austin.

Vince and Shane both thanked Austin numerous times for his heroic deed, but "Stone Cold" and Stephanie soon found out that their thanks weren't genuine. They learned that the two male McMahons were part of the evilness from the very beginning, leaving Stephanie to feel confused and hurt.

She eventually came around and forgave her dad and brother. Or did she?

She started to do things to intentionally piss off her brother and dad. One thing she's said to have done to her father, with the help of her mother, was to make Austin a 50 percent shareholder and CEO of the WWF, as each female McMahon handed over 25 percent of company stock to wrestling's meanest S.O.B. prior to the 1999 King of the Ring. She also ticked off Shane by starting a "romance" with the wrestler Test against her brother's wishes, eventually getting engaged to the ripped grappler.

She would piss the two off even further when her engagement to Test fell through and she would eventually end up the "wife" of the biggest heel in the federation, Triple H.

On November 29, 1999, the evening she was to be "married" to Test on a RAW telecast, Triple H showed up on the scene and informed Vince and a "shocked" Stephanie that she couldn't marry the grappler because she already had a "husband." Helmsley explained to everyone that on the night of Stephanie's bachelorette party he hired a bartender to fix her special drinks all night long, which eventually caused her to pass out.

The WWF's top bad guy than reveled that he drove an unconscious Stephanie to a drive-thru chapel in Vegas, where the "happy" couple ordered up a wedding for two. This dirty deed not only made Steph Triple H's wife, it also made Vince McMahon hot under the collar. But it was all in good payback, Triple H was just paying Vince back for beating him for the title on September 14 in Las Vegas.

Vince vowed to get revenge on his sneaky employee, and he also promised to clear his daughter's name, making her a single woman again. No one, especially Triple H, was going to get away with taking advantage of his darling daughter, so without hesitation Vince ordered there be a match between Triple H and himself at Armageddon. If Vince won the bout at the WWF event, Triple H would grant Stephanie an annulment, and if Triple H won the grudge match, he would not only get to stay married to the lovely lady, he would also get a shot at regaining his heavyweight title.

The "family" spat took place in Sunrise, Florida, on December 12, 1999, and just when it looked as though Vince was going to get revenge on his "son-in-law" with a sledgehammer, Stephanie stopped him in mid-swing—claiming she wanted the pleasure of doing the nasty deed. But when she hesitated in clocking her "husband," Triple H grabbed the hammer and pounded Vince unmercifully before his daughter's eyes. Then when it looked as though he was going to give her the same treatment, the two embraced, showing the whole wrestling world that they truly were a couple and that they were out to get Vince back all along for the pain he put his daughter through with The Undertaker.

Then on January 3, 2000, Stephanie added insult to injury when she stood in her "husband's" corner and cheered as she watched him defeat The Big Show to regain the world title. She would add her own title to the "newlywed" household on March 28, 2000, when she knocked off Jacqueline for the WWF Women's strap on a Smack-Down! that took place in San Antonio, Texas.

But like all the McMahons her fights were not limited to the

WWF squared circle. On October 25, 2001, Stephanie would lay the slap down on her mom, Linda, for the whole wide world to see on a SmackDown! episode, thus keeping the entire legion of WWF fans on the edge of their seats, waiting to see just what wrestling's royal family was going to do next!

Raven

While some may consider Raven a journeyman wrestler, the true description of this 6-foot-1, 237-pound grappler should be survivor. The dark warrior has done it all ever since he first came onto the wrestling scene in February 1988, as he has not only wrestled for each of the top three federations in the biz, but he has also played a major role behind the scenes as a manager, a WWF producer, and, believe it or not, behind the mic as a color commentator and a wrestling radio personality!

He has also gone by several different names during his squared-circle career. At one time or another, Raven has been known as Scotty the Body, Scott Anthony, Scotty Flamingo, and Johnny Polo. He has shown his wares all over the wrestling circuit in not only the

ECW, WCW, and WWF, but also the Global Wrestling Federation, Pacific Northwest, and the USWA.

In the early stages of his career, Raven was perfecting his moves between the ropes while also garnering titles and respect from whoever had the guts to stand across from him. He first appeared on the scene in 1988 as Scotty the Body and wrestled his first match against Jimmy Jack Funk (Jesse Barr) in Nashville, Tennessee. After less than a year in the federation, he teamed up with Top Gun to win the tag team titles on July 8, 1989, in Portland, Oregon.

A few weeks after winning his first strap, The Body and Top Gun parted ways, but would meet up again on August 8 when they faced off against each other with new partners for the tag championship. The Body wound up pinning his old teammate for his second tag title and moved on to greener pastures with his new partner in crime, The Grappler.

September 1989 would also be an important month in the young grappler's pro wrestling career, as he would win his first singles title over Carl Styles when the vacant Pacific Northwest title went up for grabs. In all he would win three singles championship belts, three tag titles, and one TV title in his time with the federation.

In 1991, he moved on to another organization, the Global Wrestling Federation, where he changed his moniker to Scott Anthony. While he moved up the ranks in no time at the GWA, as he teamed with Rip Rogers in the finals of the tag tourney in Dallas to challenge the Simpson Brothers for the title, he would eventually bolt a few months later for the WCW. There he was introduced to the wrestling fans as Scotty Flamingo.

He would make his mark in the WCW on June 20, 1992, when he beat Brian Pillman in Mobile, Alabama, for the WCW World Light-Heavyweight title. In 1993, Scotty got the opportunity to work for both of the Big Two, when he not only wrestled in the WCW, but also managed in the WWF.

He came onto the WWF scene as Johnny Polo, the goofy manager for Adam Bomb. But Polo passed his services along to Harvey Wippleman and then took on the Quebecers. While he had success managing the Quebecers, as the duo won three tag titles under Polo's guidance with the first coming on September 13, 1993, in front of millions of viewers on a Monday Night Raw, he still didn't like his WWF role. He felt his services were being grossly under utilized and his character was unappealing.

In his first go-around with the WWF, Polo got to wrestle in a handful of matches, recording his only win over Marty Jannetty. Before he left the WWF, the top promotion, he found himself in the ring with his former tag teamers, the Quebecers. Polo took on and defeated his former duo for the tag belts with the 1-2-3 Kid in a house show, proving that the teacher knew more than the students.

When the personalities in the WWF and WCW weren't panning out, the Short Hills, New Jersey, native decided it was time to move on and truly find himself in the ring. Before heading to Extreme Championship Wrestling, Philadelphia's maniacal brand of grappling, the determined warrior battled in the Mid-Eastern Wrestling Federation, where he won a singles title on April 23, 1993, in Essex, Maryland, against the Ultimate Comet during his short tenure with the company.

Then on June 20, 1995, Raven took flight, as he teamed with Stevie Richards to defeat the Public Enemy (Rocco Rock and Johnny Grunge) for the ECW World Tag Team titles. His new persona would battle in the tag ranks for a while before deciding it was time to fly the doubles coop.

When Raven decided to go it alone, he did it in typical heel fashion by turning on his former tag partner Richards, sending a message to his new federation that he would stop at nothing or nobody to get hold of the ECW World title.

After only being on the circuit seven months, Raven captured his first world title when he defeated the Sandman on January 27, 1996, in Philadelphia. He held the title for nine months until the Sandman won back the strap on October 5, 1996. But his reign didn't last very long, as Raven reclaimed the belt on December 7, 1996, from his foe. His last ECW title reign came to a close on April 13, 1997, at an ECW Pay-Per-View entitled Barely Legal.

In the summer of 1997 his first ECW tenure also came to a close when he lost a "Loser Leaves Town" match to Tommy Dreamer at Wrestlepalooza 1997. Twenty-three days later, Raven was seen ringside at a WCW Monday Night Nitro, getting his boots back on familiar ground.

In his second go-around in the WCW, Raven quickly moved up the ladder. He won the U.S. title from Diamond Dallas Page on April 19, 1998, in Colorado, starting a feud with his fellow grappler. The two Jerseyites were not only from the same state, they also had the same mentor in Jake "The Snake" Roberts. Their wars quickly became personal, as they each wanted to prove who was the better student of "The Snake."

This was also the start of a tag run with Perry Saturn and the formation of one of wrestling's most-feared gangs, The Flock, which consisted of Raven, Saturn, Kidman, Van Hammer, Scotty Riggs, Sick Boy, and Lodi. This fearless posse wreaked havoc on the WCW for quite some time under Raven's rule(s).

This lethal band of misfits eventually went their own way in the federation, and before you knew it Raven was again flying the WCW coop and wound up back in ECW for some time. He took advantage of an Eric Bischoff meeting before an August 23rd Nitro in Las Vegas, when the WCW official offered anyone on the roster a chance to walk out on their contracts if they were unhappy. Being the loner that he is, Raven stood up and walked out of the meeting and the federation without looking back.

He then inked a one-year contract with ECW two days later and wasted no time reestablishing himself in the federation, as he won the promotion's tag title on August 26, 1999, with Tommy Dreamer on a TNN broadcast. He toiled in the promotion for another year, winning another tag strap in March 2000, this time with Mike Awesome, until September 2000, returning to the WWF after his ECW contract expired.

Raven appeared on the WWF scene at an Unforgiven event during a match between Tazz and Jerry "The King" Lawler. The shaggy-haired grappler immediately caused a stir in the federation when he helped his former ECW colleague defeat "The King" by interfering in the match. Raven came to the mat and landed a DDT on Lawler, allowing Tazz to get the pin and win.

After the match, the two former ECWers formed a tag duo together, which was short-lived after taking part in a No Mercy event with the Dudley Boyz and several other top tag teams in the federation. Tazz and Raven eventually squared off against each other in a match on SmackDown!, with Raven ultimately coming out on top of the stocky Brooklyn brawler.

His next stop in the federation would again be familiar territory, as Raven would enter the WWF's Hardcore Division, the no-holds-barred region of the wrestling organization. Raven's first taste of the division came when he was picked to take part in a Triple Threat match for the Hardcore Championship with Hardcore Holly and Steve Blackman.

This was the start of some great hardcore matches. Over the course of the year, Raven not only took on top-notch talent like

Blackman, Hardcore Holly, The Big Show, Al Snow, Crash Holly, Billy Gunn, Rhyno, and Kane, he also established himself as one of the best hardcorers in the biz by winning several Hardcore championships.

While Raven will undoubtedly go down in wrestling history as one of the great grapplers who helped steer wrestling in a more violent direction, he will also go down as one of sports-entertainment's most educated men. Though his true educational background is still a mystery to this day, it is clear from his dialogue that he's an intellectual. His verbal skills on the mic are just as great as his aerial skills on the mat.

The talented grappler also wrestles with one leg that is shorter than the other and has to wear a specially made pair of wrestling boots. He also has nine tattoos and multiple piercings on his person, making him one of wrestling's true monsters of the mat.

William Regal

William Regal didn't have to travel very far to learn how to wrestle. In fact, he only had to go about 150 feet away to his grandfather Bill's house in Codsall Wood, England.

Bill Matthews was a successful professional wrestler, but his success didn't come in indoor arenas like other pro grapplers. Instead, Matthews used to work his craft at carnivals and vacation resorts in the Blackpool area and would on occasion bring his grandson along.

The young lad was so impressed with his grandfather's work that he vowed to himself to one day follow in his footsteps. Regal loved the fact that his granddad would go to these places and get paid for beating the snot out of anyone who had the guts to try and step into the outdoor ring with him.

True to his word, Regal began showing up at local carnivals at

Pleasure Beach at the tender age of fifteen trying to find a way to break into the rough and tough business. One day he got up the gumption to ask one of the promoters what was the best route for him to take in order to crack the carnival lineup and the promoter in turn informed him to challenge one of the monsters of the mat.

Not wanting to come off as scared or intimidated, Regal walked through the crowd and called out to the behemoth on hand, Magnificent Maurice. Even though he got his ass handed to him on a silver platter that day, the teenager was happy that he got the ball rolling. The ball would roll in the same direction for about another month, but with every loss came a little more confidence and ring savvy. Regal would even take up boxing and judo to help him fill out, gain strength, and build up his then-lean body.

One weekend after yet another loss, Regal caught a break when he ran into a local promoter, Bobby Barron, who liked what he saw in the determined kid, who kept coming back week after week to get his butt whipped. Being a former wrestler himself, Barron, who agreed to help train the wanna-be wrestler, sat him down and gave the young lad some advice on the dos and don'ts of the business. His only payback to the promoter would be to help his ring crew during their shows. Without hesitation, Regal jumped at the opportunity.

Regal now had to juggle his training and job with his schooling for a year, but it was a sacrifice that was well worth the effort for him, especially since it was going to bring him closer to realizing his dream of becoming a pro wrestler. In 1984, he graduated high school and was ready to give the wrestling business his full-time attention.

His first summer with Barron had him traveling up and down the coast of England, working more than fifteen shows per week. While the experience was invaluable, it was also very intimidating, as he was still a teen who was being challenged on a daily basis by the veteran warriors he was on tour with.

Pressure-packed times such as these, coupled with intense training sessions and the measly salary he was earning, had him rethinking his career choice several times over. But not all the vets were hard on the up-and-comer. At one point in their travels, Ian Wilson took the rookie under his wing and showed him how to look good between the ropes in either a win or loss.

During a seven-day TV taping, Wilson showed Regal that he had the skills to be successful on the circuit if he truly wanted it. Unlike the other seasoned wrestlers, Wilson was not only teaching Regal the basics, he was also treating him as an equal, something that didn't go unnoticed or unappreciated by the up-and-coming wrestler.

Now with a renewed vigor for the sport, the seventeen-year-old not only turned it on in Barron's promotion, he also branched out and started looking for other opportunities in the ring. While he was grateful for all Barron and Wilson had done for him, he also knew that he wanted more out of his career than to just wrestle in England.

He wanted to live the lifestyle of some of his childhood heroes like Tony St. Clair and Dave Taylor, who got to not only wrestle in the pro ranks, but also travel the world. So on he went searching for new openings and breaks and to his surprise he found one through one of his friends, Tony Francis.

Francis introduced him to Max Crabtree, a promoter who ran a wrestling organization called Dale Martin Promotions. While Crabtree didn't hire Regal right on the spot, he did do him another favor by introducing him to a talented trainer in Manchester by the name of Marty Jones.

Jones's regimen took Regal's game to another level in only a few short months and before he knew it, Regal was a regular on Crabtree's wrestling circuit. The quick learner worked the entire summer of '86 for Dale Martin Promotions and then found himself on the move once again, winding up in Brian Dixon's All-Star Promotion.

The eighteen-year-old also began working under the Steve Regal moniker while he was coming into his own at All-Star. One of the main reasons he enjoyed Dixon's promotion as compared to the others was because he was now plying his trade on foreign soil such as India, Africa, and Germany, taking on some of the world's best wrestlers.

Regal's career blossomed in 1991 and not only because of the traveling he did. The year brought the physically fit gladiator the opportunity to try out for the two biggest wrestling promotions in the world, the WWF and the WCW. Both federations went to England at different times in '91, with the WWF giving Regal his first shot to strut his stuff.

While the Connecticut-based organization didn't have any slots open for the young European, the WCW liked what they saw in him and utilized his talents for a week while they were in the country thanks to a English promoter by the name of Roig Williams.

Regal used this opportunity as a springboard to America, as he more than held his own against the WCWers during the seven-day workload in his own backyard. One year later, Bill Watts from the WCW, who remembered Regal's performance overseas, called upon him to pack his bags and come to the States to wrestle full-time for the WCW.

The talented European kicked off his wrestling career for WCW in January 1993 and five months into his stint with the federation he would be over big time with the U.S. crowd. Ordained "Lord" Steven Regal by Dusty Rhodes, the new WCWer took on any and all American grapplers on the singles circuit who dared get in the face of the English heel.

His next move up the WCW ladder came on the tag-team circuit, where he teamed with another up-and-comer, Paul Levesque, who we all know and love today as Triple H in the WWF. The duo competed for a short time as the Blue Bloods, but broke up when Levesque bolted the WCW for the WWF. Regal then formed another version of the team with Bobby Eaton and Dave Taylor. He also joined forces with major players such as Paul Orndorff, "Stunning" Steve (better know today as "Stone Cold" Steve Austin), and Ray Mysterio, Jr., but eventually found himself back on the singles turf, wrestling one-on-one. From 1993 to 1998, Regal was one of the most successful WCW grapplers, as he won 114 matches against only 84 losses.

According to a feature on Regal in the August 2001 issue of *WOW Magazine,* Regal began wrestling overseas in Japan in 1995 in between his gigs for WCW and injured himself in a match against Chris Benoit. Instead of taking time off to allow his knee to mend properly, the feature reported that Regal began taking prescription painkillers to help him cope with the pain and to also enable him to keep wrestling in the ring.

By 1996 the veteran wrestler, who had won four WCW TV titles, would not only injure himself again on the mat, his weight would skyrocket from his normal wrestling weight of 235 pounds all the way to 290 pounds. He would also be involved in a serious car accident with Benoit in Mississippi, leading to his ultimate dismissal in 1998 by the WCW.

Knowing how talented Regal was, the WWF took a chance on the out-of-work grappler a couple of months after his departure from the WCW, but Regal's hea'-h and luck would fail him again when he came down with pneumonia. After spending a week in the hospital, Regal hopped on a plane back home to try and get his health back in order.

He returned to the WWF later that summer, where management sent him to train at Dory Funk's Funkin' Dojo down in Florida so he could get into ring shape for the upcoming year. But right before he was ready to leave his training session and return to the federation, the injury bug bit again and he was out of luck for another three months with an ankle injury.

He returned to action as the "Man's Man," but that also would fail, as Regal was not only out of shape upon his comeback, he was also constantly slurring his words during his time on the microphone. The WWF reached out to their troubled star and checked him into a drug rehab center, where Regal stayed for two weeks.

But soon after his release, Regal traveled his troubled road again, forcing the WWF to ask him to reenter rehab, this time for a fourteen-week session. Regal entered the program on January 3, 1999, and during his stay, he was released by the federation, but the WWF still picked up the bill for his treatment.

When he finished his program and was free of his demons, Regal pounded the phones like he did his opponents during his career, hoping to find someone to give him another chance between the ropes. Eric Bischoff of the WCW gave him that second shot. But by the spring of 2000, Regal didn't like where his character was going in the federation and asked for his release.

Upon his release, Regal contacted the WWF and was given another go-around in Vince McMahon's federation. The WWF assigned him to one of their developmental territories in Memphis to train until they were in need of his services. On May 24, 2000, Regal proved to the wrestling world that he was on top of his game, when he took on Benoit in a match at the Brian Pillman Memorial Show in Cincinnati and put on the show of his career.

Several months later, he would make his WWF RAW debut on September 18, 2000, as William Regal in honor of his grandfather. In March 2001 Regal started out his second run in the WWF, as the goodwill ambassador of the U.K. and eventually found himself on top of the federation helping run the show as the WWF commissioner.

For seven months Regal ran the WWF like no other commissioner before him, as he helped keep the WCW/ECW Alliance in order. But in October 2001, Regal turned his back on the federation, causing Linda McMahon to hand him his pink slip as the WWF head honcho. A short time later, Shane and his sister, Stephanie, approached the foreigner about becoming the first ever Alliance commissioner, which Regal gladly accepted. The move eventually came back to bite Regal in the bum when the Alliance fell to the WWF in a battle at the 2001 Survivor Series. The former WWF commissioner had to literally kiss Vince McMahon's royal rear on national TV in order to get a job with his old boss.

Along with his commish titles, Regal also owns two WWF European championship belts. The Brit won his first strap from Al Snow on October 16, 2000, in Detroit, Michigan, and then won his second Euro title on December 4, 2000, over Crash Holly in East Rutherford, New Jersey.

The British-born grappler has overcome monstrous adversity to truly prove he belongs on the mat.

Rhyno

New faces come and go every year in the wacky world of wrestling, but one face wrestling fans all over should start getting used to is Rhyno.

This grappler came to the WWF on March 19, 2001, when he helped his good friends Edge and Christian win the tag titles over the Hardy Boyz. E&C were about to lose their championship belts to their bitter rivals, when Rhyno came from out of nowhere to spear Jeff Hardy, allowing Edge to get the pin and win.

Rhyno's monster act on that memorable March night in Albany, New York, was not performed solely to help him get over with the WWF fans. It was also done by the 285-pound bull-of-a-wrestler out of sheer loyalty for two old comrades. The three talented battlers cut their wrestling teeth together years before they came onto the WWF pro wrestling scene in Rhyno's home state of Michigan. They first met in Detroit when a young Rhyno, then known as Rhino Richards, joined a grappling gang known as Thug Life.

Thug Life was a group of wrestlers comprised of Christian Cage (WWF's Christian), Sexton Hardcastle (WWF's Edge), Joe E. Legend, and Bill Skullion, all who initially met in Winnipeg, Manitoba, on an Indian reservation out west. The foursome welcomed Rhino into their posse and immediately made their new member an honorary Canadian.

From an early age Rhyno knew he wanted to break into the wrestling business, excelling in football during his teenage years in high school as well as in the mat sport. Even though he was much slimmer in those years as compared to his thickness today, Rhyno still had the wherewithal to win state championships in wrestling in his sophomore, junior, and senior years of high school.

This was around the time he started to hit the weights with regularity and also about the time he had a growth spurt, which brought him close to the height and weight he battles at today—6-foot-2 and 275 pounds. Rhyno also contacted Scott D'Amore of Windsor and asked him to train him to become a pro wrestler and once D'Amore agreed, Rhyno was knocking heads in no time at Border City Wrestling, a Windsor-based federation that his trainer was associated with.

After tussling in the BCW for a while, Rhyno was off to lead a "Thug Life" with his Canadian friends, and then he jet-setted all over the globe knocking noggins with the best of the best from all over the world. In 1997 and 1998 he found himself often wrestling in Germany and Austria for two promoters, Pierre Williams and Otto Wanz.

While tussling overseas the still-green wrestler won several tag-team titles for the Catch Wrestling Alliance. At one time or another

Rhyno held tag gold in the CWA with either Joe E. Legend or Jean-Pierre Lafitte. On October 11, 1997, while wrestling as Rhino Richards, he and Lafitte captured the CWA tag championship from Tony St. Clair and Christian Eckstein in Hannover, Germany. Then almost a year to the day later, he and Legend beat August Smisl and Rico de Cuba for the belts on October 10, 1998. He also has fond memories of Germany because he claims to have wrestled his greatest match ever over there against Hans Shueman.

Even though he didn't win the bout with Shueman, he considered it a great accomplishment because wrestling in Germany is different from the pro style in the United States and Canada. The U.S. and Canadian version is more entertainment than sport, whereas the German version is more competitive—sort of like amateur wrestling and boxing combined. The European version also has rounds in the matches while the U.S. and Canadian doesn't.

Rhyno's championship match was also impressive not only because he and Shueman laid it all out on the line and went nine three-minute rounds that night, but also because it was his first time overseas wrestling in that style. Wrestlers and fans who were lucky enough to be there that night still talk about the action-packed match.

After Europe, it was on to Philadelphia where he contacted some of his former indie colleagues, who pulled some strings and got him a tryout with Paul Heyman, the then owner of Extreme Championship Wrestling. In 1998 Rhino even wrestled a dark match for the WWF when he took on Blair Wellington during a RAW taping in Cleveland, Ohio. But before becoming a regular for Heyman at the ECW, Rhino went back overseas where he fulfilled his commitment to work for UCW.

Once he came back to the States, particularly to the City of Brotherly Love, Rhino, who got his in-ring name from fellow wrestlers

D'Lo Brown and Scott D'Amore years back in Detroit, established himself as the fearless grappler we all know and love today.

Rhino came onto the ECW scene in 1999 and almost immediately starting using his lethal trademark move—the Gore—on everyone and anyone who got in his way. He showed everyone from the day he walked into the extreme federation that he wasn't going to back down from any challengers. As a matter of fact, he enjoyed steamrolling anybody in his path.

At one time or another, the tough-as-nails wrestler took on the likes of Tazz, Rob Van Dam, Raven, Sandman, Kid Kash, Spike Dudley, Tommy Dreamer, Yoshihiro Tajiri, and New Jack and introduced them to his noxious maneuvers.

On April 22, 2000, Rhino clashed with Yoshihiro Tajiri for the ECW World Television title in Philadelphia, Pennsylvania, and came out on top for his first ECW belt. Jealous of the young grappler's achievement, Sandman went head-to-head with Rhino for the TV strap at Hardcore Heaven '00, and wound up regretting ever entering the ring against the fierce titleholder.

On September 9, 2000, Rhino beat Kid Kash for his second ECW World Television title in Mississauga, Ontario. Rhino also successfully defended his television title against Spike Dudley at the Massacre on 34th Street later that year.

But the best was yet to come as Rhino captured the ECW World title from the Sandman in Manhattan, New York, at Guilty as Charged 2001 on Sunday, January 7. It was not only memorable because it was ECW's last Pay-Per-View as a company, it was also momentous because of the way Rhino manhandled the former ECW champ. He threatened to do bodily harm to the Sandman's wife if he didn't grant him a title shot right then and there.

The Sandman probably still regrets okaying the match as he not only lost the bout and title to the ruthless wrestler, he almost also lost his career due to the punishment handed to him that night. Rhino landed a ferocious spear and two piledrivers before getting the three-count on his fallen foe, causing the Sandman to barely escape the bout alive.

Three weeks later, Rhino inked a three-year contract with the World Wrestling Federation and made his second "unofficial" WWF debut on February 20, 2001, in a dark match prior to a Smack-Down! taping in Kansas City when he took on and beat Bo Dupp. He now officially changed his name from Rhino to Rhyno.

After making his WWF TV debut helping Edge and Christian get the win over the Hardys, Rhyno was out to make a name for himself in his new federation. He did this in stunning fashion when he faced off against another monster of the mat, Kane, on April 19 for the Hardcore title in Nashville, Tennessee, during a SmackDown! taping.

On April 30 Edge and Christian returned the favor to their former Thug Life brother by interfering in a match on RAW between Rhyno and Chris Jericho, allowing Rhyno to retain his Hardcore belt. At Judgment Day 2001 in Sacramento, California, Rhyno had another monstrous task on his hands when he took on and defeated The Big Show and Test in a three-way dance to again retain his Hardcore title.

In addition to competing for the Hardcore belt in his first few months on the WWF scene, Rhyno joined forces with his former boss, Paul Heyman, in the reformation of ECW on the July 9 edition of RAW, which took place in Atlanta, Georgia. A few weeks later, Rhyno teamed with the Dudley Boyz, Booker T, and Diamond Dallas Page along with Shane McMahon, Stephanie McMahon-Helmsley, and Paul Heyman as the WCW/ECW Alliance. They defeated the WWF squad of Kane, The Undertaker, Chris Jericho, Kurt Angle, and Steve Austin with Vince McMahon at the Invasion

Pay-Per-View held in the Gund Arena in Cleveland, Ohio, on July 22, 2001. This was also very memorable because this was the night "Stone Cold" turned his back on the WWF.

The following month would also be memorable for Rhyno, as he added a new wrestling title to his resume—the WCW United States title. He would win this belt in a match against another former ECWer, Tajiri, September 23 at the Mellon Arena in Pittsburgh, Pennsylvania, by goring the Japanese Buzzsaw and getting the pin.

In the meantime, the rest of the wrestling world better beware because there's more Gore where that came from!

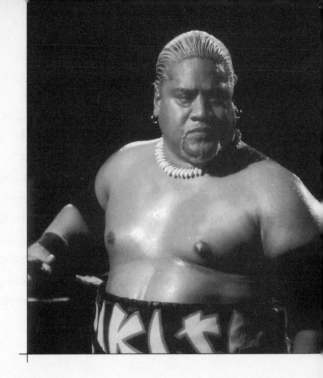

Rikishi

Rikishi is all about doing things in a *huge* way to *big* people in the federation. While many may remember Rikishi as being the driver who ran over "Stone Cold" Steve Austin at the 1999 Survivor Series, the veteran grappler has made a name for himself on the World Wrestling Federation circuit by also "butt"-ing into other wrestlers' business—no "bun" intended. One of the main ways the 401-pound giant gets in other wrestlers' faces is by using his signature move known as "the Stinkface."

"The Stinkface" is not aesthetically pleasing to watch. As a matter of fact, it's downright disgusting! The way it usually works is after Rikishi gives his opponents a pounding on the mat, the thong-wearing monster than sets up his fallen foes in one of the corners of the ring and gives them a licking of another kind when he rubs his cellulite-filled buttocks against their unfortunate faces.

Many high-profile wrestling superstars have been victims of Rikishi's facials, which is certainly something they'll never forget!

Someone who still hasn't gotten the rotten taste out of his mouth and quivers just at the thought of the horrifying moment is Edge. The talented tag-teamer and his partner Christian went up against Rikishi in a handicap match on May 4, 2000, during a SmackDown! taping in Richmond, Virginia. Not only did the duo lose to the big grappler, Edge had the pleasure of getting an up-close and personal look at Rik's rear. The disgusted wrestler is still to this day trying to remove the "egg" off his face by having facials at his local spa.

A few weeks later, Kurt Angle got a taste of what it means to be Stinkfaced. On May 22 at Judgment Day in Louisville, Kentucky, Rikishi and Too Cool squared off against the Olympic hero and Edge and Christian. The bout was full of nonstop action between the six grapplers with Rikishi's Stinkface on Angle being not only the match highlight, but also the momentum shifter. Too Cool and their jolly friend just took over the match from there, finally getting the pin and win when Grand Master Sexay nailed Edge with some aerial acrobatics, allowing Rikishi to cover the fallen wrestler for the three-count.

A little over two weeks later the trio would team up again in the ring for another six-man match, only this time it would be against Val Venis and T&A, who were also accompanied to the ring by the sultry Trish Stratus. Rikishi and his friends almost had the contest won after pounding on Test, but Venis plastered Sexay with one of Trish's leather boots, allowing his team to get the pin. Even though Too Cool and Rikishi lost the six-way tilt to Val and his pals, they would walk out of the ring smiling on June 6, as Rikishi nailed an unsuspecting Trish with—you guessed it—a Stinkface.

Another disgusting incident occurred on July 3, 2000, when Rikishi took on Triple H on RAW for the Intercontinental title. This was a wild and wacky match that had many twists and turns. At one point in the matchup, Triple H tried to land a Pedigree on his round foe, but couldn't get his hands locked to finish off the move and his opponent. Rikishi then took advantage of the missed opportunity and landed several blows in a row that included a super kick and a Samoan drop to boot. The two wrestlers ended up outside the ring trading blow after blow with Rikishi getting the better of the action. The rotund wrestler then climbed back into the ring so he could get the decision and to his surprise Chris Jericho threw Triple H back in the ring and perfectly set Helmsley up for a Stinkface. Rikishi finished off his foe and then proceeded to dance his ass off with Too Cool, who came out to celebrate with their chubby friend.

Lita was one of the next to smell what Rikishi had cooking. She took a Stinkface in a match between Jeff Hardy and Rikishi on February 22, 2001, during a SmackDown! taping in Kansas City, Missouri. After nailing his much smaller opponent with deadly moves like head butts, clotheslines, the Samoan drop, and the Banzai drop to get the win, Rikishi then cornered Lita and stink-facialed her before the crowd.

After stinking Lita, Rikishi had another opportunity to nail another WWF female personality who just so happened to be a leader of a different kind. The next lady to get a butt kissing was Stephanie McMahon, the daughter of the WWF owner. Steph received a Stinkface after a non-title match between Rikishi and Steve Austin on a RAW broadcast from New York.

Before his match on May 7, 2001, with "Stone Cold," Stephanie had been in the ring with Vince, William Regal, Mick Foley, and Rikishi. The McMahons tried to get Rik to forcefully remove Foley from the Long Island ring, but the wrestler didn't want to get involved in the squabble. Stephanie then proceeded to order Rikishi to Stinkface Foley and when he disobeyed she slapped him in the face.

The match between Austin and Rikishi would take place a little while later, with Foley sitting in the front row watching the bout and the McMahons also ringside taking in the action. During the fight, Vince jumped in the ring to try and help Austin, only to be followed by his daughter, who wanted to make sure nothing happened to her dad.

In all the confusion Austin nailed Rikishi with a stunner for the win and then tried to get a chair from outside to do some more damage on his opponent, only to involve Foley in the action. The two made their way back into the ring and while Austin was busy tussling with Foley, Rikishi took advantage of the opportunity to Stinkface Stephanie.

Not wanting to make Vince feel left out, Rikishi, with a little help from The Rock, would give the elder McMahon a Stinkface of his own on December 6, 2001, during a SmackDown! from Chicago, Illinois. Vince McMahon was supposed to kiss The Rock's ass that night after losing a previous match on RAW in which the loser of that match had to come on SmackDown! for some real ass-kissing.

McMahon would surely inhale some wind on SmackDown! from the Windy City when the Brahma Bull Rock-bottomed him to the mat and Rikishi bent over in front of him, making him literally smell what The Rock had cooking!

The Rock

The Rock burst onto the Word Wrestling Federation scene in 1996 not really knowing his role, as the fans booed and jeered the good guy wrestler, who was quickly winning big-time matches against big-time talent from the very moment he stepped through the ropes.

This situation didn't sit too well with the viewing audience, who were partial at the time to the tried-and-true veterans who had entertained them night after night over the years. The fans wanted to be able to pick their own favorites and not have a newcomer shoved down their throats. In a like manner, the proven performers were also ticked that the rookie was getting pushed into the limelight, without ever having to take his bumps on the mat before hitting the big time.

Today, six years later, the Brahma Bull has quieted all his critics. The Rock more than knows his role in the industry—as a matter of fact he's proven himself right and has held true to his words of being "the Most Electrifying Man in Sports-Entertainment." Gone are the days of the "Rocky sucks" chants from the audience, as the 6-foot-5, 275-pound gladiator now receives the biggest pop from the fans whenever he enters the ring.

While wrestling and the fans are currently his first love, several years back, before he followed in his grandfather's and dad's footsteps and became a pro wrestler, the California native had other ideas of what he'd be doing for a living. The athletically gifted youngster grew up loving sports, particulary football, in which he excelled and was recognized for at any early age.

Even though The Rock grew up in an environment that revolved around pro wrestling, as he lived in thirteen states during his childhood due to his dad's constant movement from federation to federation, he had dreams of playing in the National Football League with all of the other top gridiron greats in the United States.

During his teen years, his family settled in Bethlehem, Pennsylvania, where he tried out for and made both his high school football and wrestling teams, but only wound up staying with one squad. Even though he took on and pinned the best wrestler on campus on the very first day of practice, The Rock found amateur wrestling to be too boring for his tastes. The chiseled athlete concentrated his efforts on the full-contact sport he loved most. His choice proved to be a good one at the time, as he was voted a *USA Today* All-American football player, which in turn opened some doors for him on the collegiate level. The defensive tackle was also named one of the top fifty high school football players in the nation and eighth best in all of Pennsylvania.

He eventually wound up in the warm, sunny climate of Florida, playing football for the University of Miami. But The Rock wasn't only interested in pounding his opponents on the football field each week while he was in school, he was also there to pound the books and get an education. If his plans didn't work out with football, he would put his degree to the test and find a career in criminology, maybe even work for the government in the Secret Service. But football still seemed like an option, as he helped guide the Hurricanes to two national championships in 1989 and 1991.

But due to some injuries in his collegiate career, he was unable to play up to his full potential and went undrafted by the NFL in 1995 after graduating from Miami. Not giving up hope, the optimistic Rock took his skills across the border to the Canadian Football League, where he hooked up with the Calgary Stampeders. The American-born player figured he'd go over to the CFL, get a few seasons under his belt, make a name for himself, and eventually someone in the NFL would notice him and give him a chance.

But his U.S. citizenship would work against him in Canada, as the teams were only allowed to employ a certain number of non-Canadians on their rosters and the best the Stampeders could do for him was to place him on their taxi squad—a group that was allowed to practice with the team, but couldn't participate in league play. To make matters even worse, the job only paid him $250 a week before taxes! But he was determined to stick it out and take a run at a career in pro sports.

His football fantasy would finally come to an end when he was called by a Calgary team official who told him that he had been released from the Stampeders. One would think that The Rock would now lean on his college degree and look for a job in the subject he majored in, but even The Rock knows that crime doesn't pay. So he decided to give his dad, Rocky Johnson, a call to find out what was cooking on the pro wrestling circuit.

Rocky helped whip his son into grappling shape and taught him a thing or two about the business that he had starred in for so many years. Johnson was a former NWA Florida and WWF International champion who had made a name for himself in the wrestling world, sometimes even teaming with his eventual father-in-law, "High Chief" Peter Maivia. Growing up, the "High Chief" also taught his grandson a thing or two about how to survive in the rough and tough business, as he sometimes schooled the interested young boy on the way over to the arena before his matches.

The combination of having grown up in a pro wrestling environment, his God-given athletic ability, and a tryout from Pat Patterson, a WWF official, eventually all paid off for the pro hopeful. The third-generation grappler impressed the powers that be enough for them to offer him a developmental contract. In 1996, The Rock inked a deal and was sent to learn the ropes in the United States Wrestling Association, which was based in Memphis, Tennessee.

In no time The Rock, who first tussled under the name Flex Cavana, was not only raising eyebrows, he was also winning championships. On June 17, 1996, the quick learner and his tag partner, Bert Sawyer, defeated Reggie B. Fine and Brickhouse Brown in a tag tourney for the right to be called USWA tag team champions. Sawyer and Cavana would win the title once more before the WWF came calling.

On November 16, 1996, The Rock would leave the USWA and his Flex Cavana moniker behind for the opportunity of a lifetime to wrestle for one of the Big Two. He first entered the WWF as Rocky Maivia, a tribute ring name to both his dad and grandfather. The rookie would do both men proud in his debut, as he not only survived the Survivor Series on his first night in the federation against seasoned pros like Marc Mero, Hunter Hearst Helmsley, Jake "The Snake" Roberts, Goldust, and Jerry "The King" Lawler, but he went on to win the prestigious tournament, which made the fans and talent very unhappy.

While this win made it tough for the WWF freshman to compete in the hostile environment where fans were shouting nasty things at the baby-face grappler like "Die, Rocky, Die," he eventually made them see the light. He won them over when he turned his back on them and played the heel role, stirring up heat with not only the fans but also other wrestlers. He was now hearing the jeers in a different tone, as he was provoking the crowd and getting a reaction whenever he could. While a boo is still a boo, it's on a different level when you do something to provoke it. So by riling up the fans and getting under his foes' skin by talking smack to them, the cocky grappler was making a name for himself almost overnight in the tough-to-break-into federation.

The Rock went on to achieve new and great heights in the WWF by feuding with and winning championships from some of the top federation personalities like "Stone Cold" Steve Austin, Triple H, Mankind, Kurt Angle, Vince McMahon, and Booker T. He has also taken his WWF stardom outside the world of sports-entertainment and has done what very few wrestlers have been able to successfully do by tapping into an audience away from the ring.

The Rock has parlayed his ring success into appearances on TV shows like the MTV Video Music Awards, *That '70s Show, Star Trek: Voyager,* the Primetime Emmy Awards, *The Tonight Show with Jay Leno,* the NAACP Image Awards, *Martha Stewart Living, Late Night with Conan O'Brien,* MTV's *Total Request Live, The Rosie O'Donnell Show,* and *The View.* He also hosted *Saturday Night Live* one weekend in March 2000, bringing the show its highest ratings of the year.

The handsome wrestler's mug has also been plastered on magazines of all different types. At one time or another, The Rock's face could be found on *TV Guide, Newsweek, Entertainment Weekly, Vanity Fair, Vibe,* and *Premiere.* He was also one of the first men to ever grace the cover of the magazine *Jane.*

The WWF superstar has also found himself on a number of prestigious lists in the entertainment industry. He was voted one of *People Magazine*'s "Sexiest Men Alive" in 1999, and in 2000 *People Magazine* named him to be their "Most Intriguing" male of the year. In the same year, *Access Hollywood* cast the ring warrior as one of their "Top Ten Celebrities of 2000." In 2001, The Rock hit E! Entertainment's "Top 20 Entertainers" list, when he was penciled in at number nineteen on the popular show.

Another prestigious list "The People's Champ" has also been on is the *New York Times* Bestseller list. In January of 2000, the WWF personality released his autobiography, *The Rock Says . . . ,* which shot all the way to the number one slot during its time on the market.

The Rock has appeared on the big screen in the movie *The Mummy Returns,* as an ancient Egyptian warrior, the Scorpion King. He was so well received in that role that the studio shelled out a whopping $60 million to make a flick revolving around The Rock's character. *The Scorpion King* was released in April 2002.

There's no telling what projects the Brahma Bull will tackle next. One thing is for sure though—there is no stopping this media monster.

Saturn

Perry Saturn is one of the toughest wrestlers in the business today and it has nothing to do with his thirteen tattoos and multiple body piercings. This bald brawler got his reputation by not only pounding on and beating his opponents in the ring, but also by what he experienced in his upbringing under his own roof.

According to a feature in the September 2000 issue of *Raw Magazine,* the Cleveland native grew up in a broken home, where he was constantly told that he was a no-good loser who wouldn't amount to anything in life. Because of these harsh words Saturn grew a tough skin from a very early age, but that rough exterior couldn't keep him out of trouble as a teenager.

He was constantly in trouble with the law and his mischievous deeds landed him in and out of detention homes for the better part of his teen-hood. But ironically his saving grace came in the form of a law enforcer, Ron Turner, who took a liking to the streetwise bully.

The caring and helpful police officer made a deal with a young Saturn—if he stayed out of trouble and in school, Turner would teach him martial arts. While the future wrestling star learned kempo karate and became a black belt, he still couldn't stay out of trouble.

At Turner's urging, the seventeen-year-old enlisted himself in the army in 1984, where he aspired to become an Airborne Ranger, one of the most dangerous and respected divisions in the armed forces, along with a thousand other hopefuls. He soon found out that this wasn't going to be an easy task, as 300 wanna-be Rangers dropped out of the Airborne after only the first day.

But not Saturn. He didn't want to be known as a quitter, so he hung around and became one of the determined eighty-two who earned their wings on graduation day. Earning this degree also gave him the gumption to go after what he really wanted to be in life—a pro wrestler.

Saturn figured the army training gave him a good base to start from in his quest to become a pro grappler. He thought that if he could endure eight hours a day of basic training for thirty weeks he could withstand anything the wrestling world had to offer.

So almost immediately he began burning the phone lines calling people associated with the rough and tumble business. One such person happened to be Bill Apter, a longtime wrestling editor, who instructed the determined caller to give a buzz to Killer Kowalski, who ran a wrestling school in Boston.

Saturn took the editor's advice and dialed up Kowalski in 1988, but the legendary wrestler wasn't so receptive to training the young lad. He told Saturn, who weighed 165 pounds at the time, that he was too small to make it in the wrestling business, so he rebuffed the opportunity to train him.

Well, that's all that Saturn had to hear—another nonbeliever telling him he couldn't do something. He would not stand for being rebuffed; instead he was on a mission to become buff. So he hopped in a car almost immediately and moved close to Kowalski's gym in Massachusetts and trained hard until he got his chiseled body up to 185 pounds.

Once he got some more size, his next stop was Kowalski's door, where he showed up with the full year's tuition in hand ready to learn the ropes from the master. After seeing what the kid from Ohio did to convince him that he was truly serious about wanting to become a wrestler, Kowalski agreed to train the wrestling wanna-be.

In no time, Saturn was mastering the squared-circle maneuvers taught to him by his mentor, and by October 1990 he was making his debut for the United States Wrestling Association in Waltman, Massachusetts. He would toil around in several independent wrestling federations such as the USWA, New Japan, WAR, and the IWF for a while, learning the tricks of the trade, while hoping to one day make it in either the WWF or WCW.

His time in the indies was well spent for the green grappler, as he not only gained invaluable experience, he also picked up some championship gold along the way. He would win his first singles belt while working for the IWF as the "Iron Horseman," a wrestler who came to the ring decked out in leather from head to toe.

While toiling in the USWA, he teamed with John Kronus as the Eliminators, where the two managed to score the tag titles before they moved on to Extreme Championship Wrestling in Philadelphia, Pennsylvania. The move to ECW not only brought Saturn more gold with Kronus, it also brought him one step closer to making it to the big time.

The Eliminators were quickly establishing themselves as the best tag team in the ECW, but some were going as far as calling them the best of all time. The duo, who were known for their finishing move Total Elimination, went on to win three tag straps together in their time in the extreme federation.

In 1997 Saturn suffered an injury in the ring that put an end to a glorious tag run with Kronus and also almost ended the wrestler's career. During a match in Trenton, New Jersey, on May 31, Saturn was attempting a front kick when he tripped over a crutch that was lying in the ring, resulting in him blowing out his knee.

When he was told by the doctors that he would need a minimum of nine months to a year of recovery, Saturn again proved people wrong. He trained long and hard to get his knee back in shape and before you knew it the determined grappler was not only back on his feet, he was back in the ring in a matter of about twelve weeks.

What was even more surprising than his quick return to action was *where* he made his comeback. Saturn would come back to the wrestling scene in the City of Brotherly Love, but not for ECW. The healed wrestler came back to Philly on November 3, 1997, against Disco Inferno making his WCW debut. It was an extra special night for Saturn also because he defeated the dancing grappler in stunning fashion with his treacherous "Rings of Saturn" finishing move for the WCW TV title.

His time in the WCW was by no means a "drag"—well on second thought, maybe it was. After spending considerable time as part of Raven's Flock, where he was the enforcer of the crew, Saturn decided to break away from the group. He started a battle with another manly WCWer, Chris Jericho, which resulted in the two squaring off in a "loser has to wear a dress" match, which Jericho eventually won. While Saturn didn't do the dress any justice, no one was about to tell him how ludicrous he looked. This turned out to be a huge mistake, as the 5-foot-10, 235-pound muscle-bound wrestler continued to don the dress. After a while, Jericho even told his rival that he didn't have to wear the garment anymore, but Saturn didn't listen. He liked his Marilyn Manson–type character and plus it was getting him over with the crowd.

After Saturn came back down to earth, he teamed with Raven and made a run for tag gold. The pair would garner their first strap together against Dean Malenko and Chris Benoit on May 9, 1999. The two duos along with Ray Mysterio and Billy Kidman then had a great three-way match for the tag straps, which Saturn and Raven wound up winning.

Raven and his partner would then team with Kanyon to defend their tag titles on several occasions, only to find Kanyon turning on them a short while later to team with DDP and Bam Bam Bigelow to form The Triad. Saturn and Raven would eventually lose the straps when Saturn had to defend the belts alone due to Raven being out with an injury. A little over one month later, Saturn would win the belts back again, only this time with another partner, Chris Benoit, a former foe.

Benoit and Saturn hooked up on June 7, 1999, much to the dismay of Ric Flair, when the "Nature Boy" walked out on Benoit during a title match against Diamond Dallas Page and Bam Bam Bigelow and Saturn filled in. The two beat Bam Bam and DDP, but Flair was able to reverse the decision, pulling rank as president of the federation at the time.

Showing that their initial win was no fluke, Saturn and Benoit again whooped Bigelow and Page three days later on Thunder, but would lose to the twosome three nights later at the Great American Bash. The two then teamed with Dean Malenko and Shane Douglas and formed The Revolution, a havoc-wreaking heel group.

Currently, Saturn has found himself 'rassling with the big boys, as he plies his trade in the WWF taking on any and all who come his way. His WWF tenure started back on January 15, 2000, when the WCW's head booker was let go by the federation. Saturn, along with Eddie Guerrero, Benoit, and Malenko all saw this as an opportunity of a lifetime and asked for their release from the organization.

Once granted their release the foursome wasted no time signing on with the WWF. On June 31, the four men made their first appearance for the WWF on a RAW Is War broadcast and stole the show, as they started a feud with the WWF's most popular posse, DX.

In his short time since arriving on the WWF scene, Saturn has already made his presence known by winning both the European and Hardcore titles. From his troublesome days as a teen to his WWF days as a superstar, this monster has come a long way.

Al Snow

Over the years, many have tried and many have failed to get into Al Snow's head, but when push comes to shove they all find out the same thing—this guy's one hell of a wrestler. The Lima, Ohio, native became a grappling fan at the age of fourteen and from that moment on he was hooked.

Snow grew up watching the Original Sheik, and as soon as he graduated from Lima Senior High School he began looking for a wrestling school where he could learn the trade. His pursuits and efforts landed him an opportunity to learn from the Anderson brothers in North Carolina, who were a twenty-four-hour bus trip away. But the determined Snow didn't care about the distance, as he sold his 1968 Dodge Monaco in order to have enough money to make the trip. He would learn sooner rather than later that the wrestling business was not all fun and games.

From the moment he stepped off his day-long bus ride to North Carolina, Gene Anderson put Snow through a rigorous training session to see if he had both the mental and physical makeup to someday make it between the ropes. When the eager student didn't fare well in his tryout, the Andersons put him back on a bus with all his belongings—plus the black-and-blues he received from his ring sessions—and advised Snow to take up a new career interest.

Down but not out, Snow returned home and found an instructor, Jim Lancaster, who was willing to teach him the ins and outs of pro wrestling. Almost immediately, Lancaster liked what he saw in Snow. Unlike the Andersons, the wrestling teacher thought Snow had great potential to be a solid performer in the ring, as he not only had a love for the business, but also the athletic background and ability to back it up.

The gifted athlete held a black belt in kempo karate and a brown belt in jujitsu and had studied kung fu and Muay Thai, so taking bumps in a not-so-fancy gym on a concrete floor only covered by a flimsy tumbling mat wasn't going to be so hard. Snow just needed to find someone who believed in his abilities and that person was Lancaster.

Snow's first decade in the wrestling business had him toiling in the independent promotions all over the world as various different grappling personalities. In 1983 he first started out in his home state of Ohio, where he wrestled as one half of the Texas Chain Gang in Springfield. From there he moved around a lot and took on opponents in places such as St. Louis, Minneapolis, and Plymouth, Indiana.

The reason the green grappler moved around so much for so long was because he was trying to make a name for himself and get recognized by one of the talent scouts from the Big Two. And if nothing else, Snow did make a name—as a matter of fact he made many names—for himself.

At one time or another during his career Snow was part of the Fantastics, the Sensationals, the Motor City Hitmen, the Wild Bunch, the New Fabulous Kangaroos, the Dynamic Duo, and the Rockers. He also wrestled as Steve Moore, Shinobi, Avatar, and Leif Cassidy.

In the spring of 1990, Snow found himself in the GWA, where he was one half of the Wild Bunch with Machine Gun Mike Kelly. The duo was very popular in the federation because they were the only baby-face team on the circuit, which immediately resulted in their becoming fan favorites. Kelly and Snow not only parlayed their popularity on the mat into five tag-team championships, the twosome also appeared as extras in the 1993 movie *Rudy*, about a boy from a steel-mill town who wanted to play football for Notre Dame.

Rudy was a perfect flick for Snow to be a part of, as the lead character on-screen played by Sean Astin resembled his real-life wrestling persona. The two had similar problems and obstacles to overcome, and through their drive and perseverance they were able to achieve their lifelong dreams, even though others consistently mocked their goals.

His wrestling career not only got him movie roles, it also afforded him the luxury to travel overseas and experience life and wrestling outside the United States. Snow had the opportunity to wrestle in Japan for promotions such as Kitao Pro and WAR. While abroad, Snow tussled with grapplers such as Takashi Okanwara, Tatsumi Kitahara, Ishinriki, Sabu, and Chris Benoit.

In 1993 Al gained some invaluable ring experience in the WWF when he worked as a jobber known as Steve Moore. While it's the job of a jobber to help make his better-known ring rival get over with the crowd, Snow didn't care as he not only was getting to wrestle against some stiff competition like The Undertaker, Marty Jannetty, and The Smoking Gunns, he was also getting exposure to the worldwide WWF fans.

With so much wrestling under his belt, Snow finally made an impression in Jim Cornette's Smoky Mountain Wrestling in 1995. He came onto the circuit and teamed with the Unibomb (today known as Kane) and together the two would turn the tag region upside down. They feuded mostly with the federation's top duo, the Rock 'n' Roll Express. After a four-month battle, Snow and his newfound partner would dethrone the champs and keep the title of SMW Tag champions for a three-month stint of their own before losing the straps to The Thugs in the summer of '95.

When Smoky Mountain went under later in 1995, Snow got a chance to work full-time for a while at his prestigious wrestling school in Cleveland known as Bodyslammers. But the veteran grappler didn't only extend his knowledge to help train up-and-coming wrestlers, he also found himself training Dan Severn for the Ultimate Fighting Championship, where unlike wrestling, the action and punches were real.

Also in 1995 the World Wrestling Federation came calling. Snow came onto the WWF and immediately made an impression, but it wasn't a good one. He first wrestled under the moniker of Avatar, a multicolored masked wrestler, who didn't go over well with the fans at all.

After only a couple of weeks on the scene, Snow ditched the Avatar persona, but not the mask, and began wrestling as Shinobi, a ninja-type character. Well, needless to say he wasn't popular as a ninja either. So the third time's a charm, right?

Wrong! Snow decided to take wrestling fans back to the '70s when he appeared on the mat circuit as Leif Cassidy, a wrestler who was a cross between 1970 teen idols Leif Garrett and David Cassidy. It was bad enough that Snow had to enter the ring as this character, but poor Marty Jannetty also had to be subjected to this freak, because Cassidy was one half of a wrestling tag team known as The New Rockers. While The New Rockers were a great comic relief at times in the ring, they were never taken seriously enough to last.

Heartbroken over his three strikes in the ring, Snow went over to Extreme Championship Wrestling in 1997 on loan from Vince McMahon and the WWF and ultimately found himself (and a head) as a wrestler. While Snow claims that he almost immediately began hearing voices from a woman's mannequin head he found one night after an ECW match, which he simply named Head, he credits his good friend Mick Foley with helping him come up with his gimmick.

"I can't believe I'm actually going to say this, but Mick [Foley] actually had a hand in it," Snow said in an interview with *Wrestling Digest* in August 2000. "He and I were riding down the road one day and I had the Styrofoam head with me. He put a mask on it with a wig and the idea came to get a human-like head. When I took it to ECW, guys like Mikey Whipwreck and Spike Dudley really helped it catch on with the fans."

The act was so popular that WWF head honcho Vince McMahon wanted Snow back in his federation. While Snow was all smiles about "heading" back to the WWF, he soon would become frustrated again with his role in the federation, as again he found himself to be a jobber instead of a "headliner."

So, after some soul-searching and some energizing conversations with Head, Snow decided to start his own wrestling gang known as the J.O.B. Squad, which included himself and fellow jobbers at the time, Bob Holly, The Blue Meanie, 2 Cold Scorpio, and Duane Gill.

Along with his new crew and his better-looking Head, Snow could now be found entering the arena sporting a J.O.B. Squad

T-shirt, which had the slogan "Pin me . . . pay me!" written across the back—letting everyone around the wrestling globe know that even though he was losing, he was still happy to be getting a paycheck for doing what he loved.

Little by little Snow began earning more than just cash. He started getting some respect and recognition with his new group, and his next stop was the WWF's newly created Hardcore division, which resembled the no-holds-barred style of grappling that went on at ECW.

Snow went on to thrive in the more violent ring atmosphere and has captured the strap an impressive five times in his crazy career, earning the distinguished right to be called "The Crown Prince of Hardcore." He first won the title from Bob Holly at a Backlash event on April 25, 1999, in Providence, Rhode Island.

Snow is also the holder of one European championship title and one tag-team championship strap. He won his only Euro title on September 1, 2000, in Louisville, Kentucky, against the bald brawler Saturn. His tag team title came on November 2, 1999, in Philadelphia when he and Mankind beat the Hollys.

Because of his training background and skill level, the veteran grappler was chosen to be one of the official trainers for *WWF Tough Enough*, a wrestling reality show that aired on MTV in 2001. When he's not training or wrestling, Snow can be found collecting hockey jerseys. It's been a passion of his for almost two decades and he currently owns over 130 sweaters from teams all over the world. Snow sometimes shows off some of his collection to his fans on the road when he enters the arena donning his jersey of choice. He'll usually wear the hometown team's colors of the city he's working in, but don't bet against this cuckoo-for-Cocoa-Puffs wrestler wearing the jersey of the home squad's biggest rival either. It all depends upon what's in his (or her) head that night.

Lance Storm

Unlike most pro wrestlers, Lance Storm didn't grow up dreaming about becoming a king of the ring. Instead, the Sarnia, Ontario, native who excelled in both academics and athletics in high school, had every intention of going to college, getting his degree, and taking on the suits of the business world.

While attending West Ferris Secondary School in Canada, Storm, who began lifting weights at the age of thirteen, was an athletic scholar. He competed in track and field, basketball, and volleyball, while managing to graduate with a 89.5 average. After high school, the gifted student then moved on to Wilfred University in Waterloo, Ontario, where he enrolled in the honors business program and played volleyball for the Golden Hawks.

But after only a year and a half at Wilfred, Storm lost his desire to stay in school when he began butting heads with his volleyball coach, which in turn took the fun out of the game for him. The young athlete felt that if he couldn't play volleyball—one of his passions—he had no reason to stay enrolled at the university, so he dropped out.

The knocking heads was a sign of things to come. After some serious thinking, Storm decided to pack his bags in June 1990 and move to Calgary and enroll in another university. But this school, the Hart Brothers Pro-Wrestling Camp, also known as the Dungeon, was more about brawn than brains.

The 5-foot-11, 225-pound Storm chose the Dungeon as his place of training not only because it was founded and run by the legendary Stu Hart, but mainly because the school had produced countless other wrestlers of his size who went on to successful careers around the wrestling world. Wrestlers like Chris Benoit, Brian Pillman, Jim "The Anvil" Niedhart, Davey Boy Smith, and of course Owen and Bret "The Hitman" Hart all got their starts at the famous training grounds.

At this school of hard knocks, Storm was trained primarily by Keith Hart, who taught him everything he needed to know about the grappling business. Under Hart's tutelage, the former business student was training five days a week for three grueling hours a day with other aspiring wrestlers.

Three months after moving to Calgary, Storm was ready for action. He made his pro debut with the Canadian Wrestling Connection in Ponoka, Alberta, on October 2, 1990, against none other than his classmate Chris Jericho, who would later become his tag-team partner. Neither Hart student would come out victorious in the match on this night, as they wrestled to a fifteen-minute draw. But Storm would get his first taste of victory later on in the night when he competed in a battle royal bout in the main event, and won.

This was the start of a wrestling career that would see the young brawler compete around the globe for some of the most prestigious federations in the business. Storm at one time or another wrestled for Stampede Wrestling, WFWA (IWA), Canadian Rocky Mountain Wrestling, FMW, CWA, Smoky Mountain Wrestling, and WAR.

In February of 1997, Storm caught a big break when Extreme Championship Wrestling signed him on to work for the Philadelphia-based promotion. There the talented grappler not only got to work with wrestlers such as Bam Bam Bigelow, Rob Van Dam, Chris Candido, Shane Douglas, the Dudley Boyz, and Justin Credible, he also took home the tag-team belt three times during his run with the federation.

In June 2000, his ECW career came to a close when World Championship Wrestling came calling. In the summer of 2000, the Canadian-born wrestler came over to WCW and almost overnight went from being an even-tempered performer to becoming one of the most popular heels in the promotion.

Storm was not only taking titles from his foes, he was also re-naming the belts he was winning after his beloved country. For example, in July he captured the United States Championship in a tournament bout against Buff Bagwell, Shane Douglas, and Mike Awesome and changed the title name to the Canadian Heavyweight Championship.

One week later on July 24, the Heavyweight title holder took on Big Vito for the Hardcore Championship and changed the name of the belt to the Saskatchewan Hardcore International title after beating his opponent.

But he wasn't finished there. A few days later Storm took on and defeated Lt. Loco for the cruiserweight title and switched the name of the strap to the 100 Kilos and Under Championship, becoming the first WCW wrestler to hold three championship belts simultaneously.

Less than one year later, Storm's contract was picked up by the World Wrestling Federation, which had also just purchased WCW from AOL Time Warner Inc. Storm made his first appearance on the WWF scene on April 1, 2001, in Houston, Texas, at WrestleMania X7 in the Houston Astrodome. The new WWF employee was seated in a skybox along with several other WCW ring personalities cheering on their new boss, Shane McMahon, who was taking on his father, Vince, in a Streetfight match. Storm would later pop up on May 28 on a RAW Is War show and interfere in one of Perry Saturn's matches, thus paving the way for other WCWers to get in on the TV action.

Storm, along with Mike Awesome, would also break new ground on July 9 when they became the first two WCW grapplers to join forces with a new ECW group headed by Paul Heyman and Stephanie McMahon. His first win with the federation would be a big one, as he defeated the WWF's Albert to become the new Intercontinental champion, marking the first time any wrestler from another promotion held that title.

Storm has currently shed his anti-American act, but he still remains one of sports-entertainment's most talented wrestlers due to his assortment of ring skills and also for his sharp tongue on the mic. His "If I can be serious for a moment" mantra has taken him further in the wrestling world than he ever could have imagined.

Trish Stratus

T rish Stratus is all about meeting life's challenges and overcoming obstacles, while shocking a few people along the way.

At first glance people unfamiliar with her background would never guess that this 5-foot-4 blond beauty is in the World Wrestling Federation because of her mat skills, but what they don't know can hurt them—especially in this case.

Stratus grew up in a Toronto household that had her playing soccer at the age of three. But the athletically gifted diva also has a fitness model background, which had her in the gym training six days a week to sculpt an already fit body.

Believe it or not, she didn't originally intend on becoming a model. During a professor's strike at York University, where Stratus was studying biology and kinesiology, she was approached by the publisher of *MuscleMag International,* Robert Kennedy, to do a photo shoot even though she had no prior modeling experience.

She so impressed Kennedy during her first shoot with her looks and her ease in front of the camera that he offered her a career in the tough-to-break-into industry, where the magazine would use her exclusively as their headliner and head-turner! She first appeared in *MuscleMag International* in a feature in the May 1998 issue and four months later her first cover shot graced the stands all across the globe.

But a short while after her first successful shoot, the strike at school ended and she now faced the tough task of juggling her studies along with her booming modeling career. Stratus tried doing both for a while, but soon realized that she had to make a choice. Both demanded so much of her time that she couldn't possibly keep burning the candle at both ends without one of her interests suffering, so she decided to put school aside for some time in order to focus on her blossoming career.

The celebrity on the rise made a few guest appearances on the Canadian talk show *Off the Record,* which would eventually help land her a job with the WWF. Every time Stratus was scheduled to appear on the show, she was alongside a federation star, which started stirring up Internet rumors that she was WWF bound.

Even though there was no truth to the matter, Stratus saw an opportunity before her to break into a new industry—the wrestling world. This idea so intrigued her, as she grew up in Toronto watching the WWF religiously as a child, that she then went out and hooked up with a grappling radio show to try and open up some eyes in the industry.

Her game plan eventually panned out when one night after a fitness show in the Toronto area, she was approached by Terry Taylor from the WWF, who wanted to help her fulfill her dream of becoming a pro wrestler. Almost immediately Stratus took it upon herself to get ready to rumble. She enrolled in Sully's Gym in Toronto to be trained by the world-famous Ron Hutchinson, who had a knack for getting his students ring-ready.

She trained at Sully's for six long, hard months, sometimes being the only woman in the gym, under the guidance and tutelage of the famous wrestling trainer. At first the Canadian Hall of Fame wrestler was reluctant to take on Stratus as a student, but once he saw her in action he knew she was tough enough to take her licks on the mat.

She made her WWF TV debut on March 19, 2000, on Sunday Night Heat, where she immediately showed interest in Test, but the next night on RAW she formally introduced herself to the wrestling world alongside the grappler and his partner, Albert, to form the eyebrow-raising tag team known as T&A.

She began turning heads and pissing off other wrestlers almost immediately with her good looks and interfering ways. She not only helped T&A defeat the destructive Dudley Boyz, she also helped Shane McMahon get a victory over The Big Show by interfering in their bout.

She made her in-ring debut in Memphis, Tennessee, alongside T&A to take on and defeat Lita and the Hardy Boyz on June 20, 2000. A short while later she was up to her interfering tricks again when she distracted Rikishi long enough for Val Venis to walk away with a win and the Intercontinental belt around his waist.

Speaking of waist, Trish doesn't "waist" any time if an opportunity presents itself to "hook up" with the right people. For a couple of months she was involved with a story line that revolved around her and the WWF owner, Vince McMahon, putting her front and center in the wrestling world after only being with the company for less than a year.

And if that wasn't impressive enough, the buxom blond would win the WWF Woman's title at the 2001 Survivor Series when she was the last female left standing in a six-woman Battle Royal that included Mighty Molly, Jazz, Jacqueline, Ivory, and Lita.

How the immensely talented Canadian beauty will shock the world of sports-entertainment next only the wrestling gods (and Vince McMahon) know for sure.

Tajiri

The World Wrestling Federation knows no boundaries when it comes to finding the top wrestling performers around the globe. Vince McMahon wants his federation to be known worldwide as the place where all the best in the business come to wrestle and you need to look no further than Tajiri to know that this is the truth.

The 5-foot-9, 205-pound grappler was born on September 29, 1970, in Japan, the land of the rising sun, and would soon become a rising star in America as a member of the WWF. He grew up in his native country idolizing all the legendary wrestlers that came before him like Rikidozan, Shohei "Giant" Baba, and Tiger Mask.

But the warrior he most looked up to was Killer Khan. The young hopeful loved the way this grappler performed in the ring so much that he adopted the spraying of a blinding mist gimmick into his arsenal just like Khan used to do when he was in trouble in a match.

Tajiri was trained in Japan by Kendo Nagasaki and made his pro debut with the International Wrestling Association on October 16, 1994, against El Gran Apache. After a year of wrestling on the Japan circuit where he honed his martial arts skills and wrestling fundamentals, he traveled across the globe for a title shot.

The eager gladiator traveled to the United States on June 24, 1995, for a chance at the NWA/IWA heavyweight title against Dan Severn and his countrymen wouldn't be disappointed as he returned home from Williamsport, New Jersey, with the title belt draped around his waist.

After returning home to grapple on the Big Japan Pro Wrestling card for a while, he again took to the air and traveled to Mexico, where he landed in the Empresa Mexicana de Lucha Libre territory. Tajiri donned a mask during his stay in Mexico and not only won the EMLL Light-Heavyweight strap over Dr. Wagner, Jr., on July 19, 1996, as Aquarius, but more importantly, he learned how to use the entire ring and ropes. This is where he learned the aerial acrobatics that we all know and love him for today.

The next major federation that helped mold Tajiri into the wrestler he is today is Extreme Championship Wrestling. The ripped athlete first came on the Extreme scene on December 11, 1998, when he stood toe-to-toe with Antifaz Del Norte. The ECW wrestler may not have known who this new guy was before the bout, but once Tajiri whipped his butt, Del Norte got to know him up-close and personal.

If nothing more, Tajiri learned how to brawl during his time in ECW. Night after night the Japanese wrestler was slated to wrestle in matches where the odds weren't in his favor, but he didn't care. As a matter of fact he loved wrestling against the odds.

For instance, on September 19, 1999, Tajiri took part in a three-way dance match with Little Guido and Jerry Lynn and walked out a winner at the Anarchy Rulz event. Then on April 8, 2000, the young gun again took on Lynn and Guido in a trio dance and would not only defeat his opponents that night, he would also strut away with the ECW TV title. As if two other foes weren't enough of a challenge for the acrobatic wrestler, on July 16, 2000, at Heatwave in Los Angeles, Tajiri went up against Mikey Whipwreck, Psicosis, and Little Guido in a four-corners match and again ended up victorious.

In January 2001, the Japanese Buzzsaw signed a letter of intent to work for the WWF and a few months later he made his official federation debut on an episode of SmackDown!, speaking in Japanese and bowing to the WWF commissioner William Regal.

On July 19 Tajiri showed the WWF audience that he can do more than just speak his language and fetch tea for the commish. He teamed with the bad-ass brawler, The Undertaker, and his ferocious brother, Kane, that night on SmackDown! against the dreaded and dangerous Dudley Boyz and Tazz. The four-eyed warriors and their stumpy friend would learn the hard way that they were no match for Tajiri and the Brothers of Destruction.

The following month Tajiri would find federation gold when he defeated X-Pac on August 6, 2001, in Anaheim, California, on RAW, becoming the WWF Light-Heavyweight champ. The WWF/ECW/WCW merger also proved to be good to Tajiri, as he took on and beat Kanyon on September 10 for the WCW United States Championship. In October, Tajiri made it three months in a row that he won a title, when he squared off against Kidman and beat his foe for the WCW Cruiserweight strap in Kansas City, Missouri.

This monster from Japan seems capable of almost anything—he could probably even take down Godzilla himself.

Tazz

When the creators of the wrestling reality show, *WWF Tough Enough,* were drawing up the plans for their new show, they knew they needed to hire pro wrestlers as trainers who were going to not only give the contestants a fair chance to become pro wrestlers, but who also were going to be able to make them *tough enough* to survive on the mean mats of the highly competitive industry.

Just by taking a look at his background and appearance, the producers knew they had one of the best guys for the job in Tazz. The bald warrior stands in at 5-foot-9 and weighs in at a solid 250 pounds. He was also born and raised in Brooklyn, New York, on some of the meanest and thuggish streets in the world where only the strong survived.

The future WWF superstar was athletically gifted as a child, excelling on the football field and wrestling mat growing up, as well as being a star student in the local dojo, where he mastered the art of judo. As he was growing up, people, especially his judo teacher, would tell him that he should pursue a career in wrestling. The stocky Brooklynite not only left an impression on them with his size and athletic skills, but he also sported a mohawk at this time in his life.

When he was old enough to make a career choice, he followed his heart and decided to take a chance on trying to become a pro wrestler, even though he knew there was going to be a hard road ahead of him. His dad helped get him started on the right foot by getting Tazz enrolled in a wrestling training program run by Johnny Rodz.

The school turned out to be the best training grounds for the wrestling wanna-be, as Rodz's class only had two other students, Big Dick Dudley and Damien Demento. Tazz was able to get up-close and personal training from the instructor, which helped him learn the ropes a lot quicker.

After finishing his training, he traveled south of the border to Puerto Rico to make his pro debut on June 3, 1987. From there he traveled the world looking for work on the independent circuit, trying to catch someone's eye from the Big Two who was willing to give him a shot to show his skills. His big break came when he was wrestling on a card one night for Smoky Mountain Wrestling and Paul Heyman from the WCW happened to be in attendance. The two hit it off immediately and Heyman promised Tazz he would try to get him on the WCW roster.

Heyman's efforts initially failed as Tazz never graced the WCW mats while he was there, but once he started his own promotion, ECW, Tazz was one of the first wrestlers to get a phone call. The New York–born wrestler made his debut in the Philadelphia-based federation in October 1993, and before he left the extreme promotion in 2000, he would garner three championship titles to add to his wrestling resume.

By winning the tag strap, the World TV title, and the World Heavyweight Championship, Tazz became one of only a handful of distinguished ECWers to ever hold all three belts in their careers.

He then made his way to the WWF, where he debuted at Royal Rumble 2000 on his hometown turf of New York City in Madison Square Garden. In his first-ever WWF match, Tazz took on and defeated an up-and-coming wrestler at the time, Kurt Angle. His first victory was impressive because not only did he beat a former Olympic gold medalist, he also put an end to Angle's WWF winning streak. Angle came into the match at MSG undefeated, but left New York a broken man in more ways than one after his bout with the monstrous Tazz.

Triple H

In the bizarre world of professional wrestling, where anything can happen at a moment's notice, there has been one constant element through the years—good vs. evil. While the good guys, or baby faces as they're known today, had always gotten the glory, the bad guys, or heels, constantly were being overlooked—until Triple H came into the picture.

The four-time WWF champion came over from the WCW in 1995 and made his federation debut in May as the snobbish grappler, Hunter Hearst Helmsley, but he was far from ready to be sports-entertainment's top bad boy. The rude, crude warrior found out the hard way that success and championships weren't handed to you in the WWF, you had to earn your stripes before you got a chance to get over with the crowd and wear federation gold.

Helmsley, like every grappling great before him, had to climb the ladder of success before he got his chance at a major push. The rich blue blood from Greenwich, Connecticut, took on mid-carders such as Bob Holly, Fatu, Doink, and Duke Droese, and held his own, but when WWF officials tried to move him up to the next level against talent like Bret Hart and Razor Ramon, he failed miserably. Some were even questioning his ability to compete with the top-notch federation performers.

But HHH took matters into his own hands and showed the wrestling world that he wasn't afraid to get dirty—literally—in order to find success on sports-entertainment's top circuit. The determined wrestler took on WWF country boy, Henry Godwin, and from the beginning the feud was very entertaining. HHH was the clean-shaven, snobby city boy who walked around with his nose in the air, while Godwin was a hick from the sticks who went around dumping buckets of slop on his opponents.

Their bouts eventually led to the famous "Hog Pen" match at an In Your House event in late 1995, which saw Helmsley surprisingly come out on top despite wrestling in unfamiliar elements. The match called for HHH and Godwin to square off in a hog pen, mud and all, which immediately gave the home-field advantage to the down-and-dirty farmer.

But HHH went hog-wild at the conclusion of the match. Godwin, who connected on a few Irish whips and sent his opponent face first into the slop, went home squealing after the match. HHH eventually scored the pin and win over his mud-loving foe. The victory over the country bumpkin put Helmsley on the road to WWF stardom.

Even though he lost his next big match to Duke "The Dumpster" Droese at the January 21, 1996, Royal Rumble event in Fresno, California, Helmsley would benefit. The "Free for All" bout against Droese in Selland Arena was a stipulation match—the winner would enter the Royal Rumble that night with the desired Number 30 slot, while the loser would enter the kill-or-be-killed bout with the dreaded Number 1 position.

While many thought Helmsley would be eliminated almost immediately because he entered the ring first in the thirty-wrestler event, he shocked the wrestling world by staying alive longer than any of the other twenty-nine participants, until he was ousted at the forty-eighth-minute-and-one-second mark of the Rumble by Diesel. HHH again opened up some eyes as he was able to hold his own and do battle with some of wrestling's big names at the time, such as Bob Backlund, Jerry "The King" Lawler, Jake "The Snake" Roberts, Yokozuna, Savio Vega, Vader, Owen Hart, Shawn Michaels, Diesel, the Ring Master (Steve Austin), Issac Yankem (Kane), Marty Jannetty, and the British Bulldog.

Helmsley was quickly becoming a hit with both the male and female fans, as the 6-foot-4, 246-pound grappler had something for everyone. The women enjoyed his chiseled physique and good looks, while the men enjoyed his mat skills and the bevy of beautiful women who escorted him to the ring.

While most ladies loved HHH, there was one gorgeous gal who began to dislike the evolving wrestler. Her name was Rena Mero, soon to be known on the wrestling circuit as Sable, and she was one of the pretty valets who accompanied Helmsley to the ring each night. But when the grappler started losing matches, he began taking his frustrations out on his stunning blond escort for the whole viewing audience to see. These actions set the stage for a bitter feud between Helmsley and another WWF newcomer, "Wildman" Marc Mero, who just so happened to also be Rena's real-life husband.

On March 31, 1996, HHH made his first appearance at the ultimate wrestling show, WrestleMania. The excited Helmsley took on the Ultimate Warrior that night at WrestleMania XII in front of a sold-out crowd in Arrowhead Pond in Anaheim, California, but his excitement would turn to embarrassment in no time flat. He lost in humiliating fashion to the war-painted grappler in one minute and forty-three seconds and blamed Sable for the loss.

Enter the "Wildman," who had grown sick and tired of Helmsley's treatment of the lovely lady, starting a war of more than just words between the two grapplers. Rena turned her back on HHH and now came in on the arm of her hubby, forming one of the best one-two combos in the wrestling business at the time. The duo would garner championship gold together, as Rena guided her better half to the Intercontinental Championship, enraging Helmsley who was yet to win any kind of title in the WWF.

But Helmsley's evil heel ways took over when it was time to get revenge on the Meros. The sneaky gladiator called upon "Mr. Perfect" Curt Hennig, who had been away from the WWF for three years, to become his manager. Together the two evildoers came up with a plan that put the "Wildman" on the losing end of a match.

The heelish pair plotted to make everyone believe that their partnership was on its way out. Hennig began taking several of his wrestler's female valets and disappeared with them mid-match, as Helmsley was battling his opponents. Appearing to be livid, HHH dared Hennig to take him on in a match on October 21, 1996, on a Monday Night RAW to settle their differences. Of course, the in-cahoots manager agreed.

But before the match could even take place, Helmsley slammed a cart into Hennig's knee, causing the manager to fake an injury and claim he couldn't take part in a grudge match that night. Enter Hennig's good buddy, Marc Mero, who then offered to fill in for the injured challenger.

When approached with the idea of Mero taking Hennig's place, Helmsley would only agree to tussle with the "Wildman" if he put his Intercontinental belt on the line. Mero unknowingly agreed to the terms and HHH went on to win his first belt ever in typical heel-like fashion, as the fix was in when Helmsley nailed Mero with his lethal Pedigree move to gain the IC title.

Mr. Perfect soon left the WWF for the WCW, so HHH set his sights on another manager—Marlena. She just so happened to be employed by and married to another WWF superstar, Goldust. When his heelish efforts didn't pay off this time, he turned to Curtis Hughes to be his new ring escort. But because of health reasons, Hughes had to give up his post as Helmsley's sidekick, causing the WWF wrestler to look elsewhere.

Helmsley immediately thought of a great person to hire for the vacancy, Joanie Laurer, a.k.a. Chyna. The well-built and pretty female wrestler had gone to the same wrestling school as HHH, and he thought she would be great for the role. The gorgeous grappler would not only make him look good coming into the ring, but she could also serve as his bodyguard, dispelling any and all sneak attacks on the WWF warrior.

The Ninth Wonder of the World earned her wings and was hired on the spot one night when she attended one of Helmsley's matches. He was up against The Rock, yet Goldust and his wife, Marlena, decided to interfere in the bout.

Chyna immediately darted up from her front-row seat and began pouncing the Golden One's wife in front of a stunned wrestling audience. In the next few months, the 5-foot-9, 185-pounder not only watched HHH's back, but she also guided him to a King of the Ring title and a European Championship. Chyna also became a key acquisition for Helmsley because she helped the WWF's rising star, along with Shawn Michaels, form one of the federation's most popular heel groups, D-Generation X.

The group, which was at first led by Michaels and then by Helm-

When he returned to wrestling in January 2002, Triple H proved to wrestling fans all over the world that he's still got "game."

Team Xtreme is famous
for their high-flying moves
and kickass attitude.

Black Jack Brown

Black Jack Bro

Black Jack Brown

His ring rivals may not believe that
the Olympic gold medalist is the greatest wrestler ever,
but Kurt Angle himself will insist "it's true."

Hunter is a full-blooded wrestling superstar—
and he's got the Pedigree to prove it.

Y2J will tell anyone to "shut the hell up" if they try and stop him from winning any more championships.

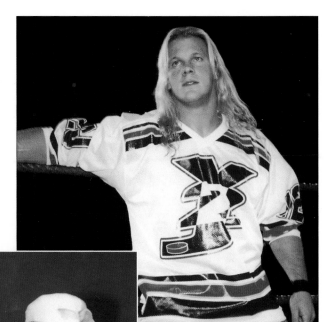

Black Jack Brown

Rob Van Dam flexes the muscles that helped him remain ECW champion for twenty-three months straight, a record for the extreme federation.

Howard Kernats

Rhyno is just as determined to get some championship gold now,
as he was back when he was Rhino.

While The Rock is still "The People's Champion," many people didn't know which way to cheer when the NWO ganged up on him and Hulk Hogan painted the NWO's logo on the Brahma Bull's back during a RAW event in February 2002.

The Texas Rattlesnake is going to need
the whole six-pack once this match is over.

sley, wreaked havoc on not only the WWF wrestlers, but also the upper-management team, who had no idea how to control these out-of-control personalities. DX helped change the face of wrestling forever. The posse, which at first consisted of HHH, Chyna, Michaels, and the late, great Rick Rude, was known for their lewd, crude, and boorish behavior. The loud crowd, who loved to tell people to "Suck it!," constantly interfered in matches, mooned, crotch-chopped, and cursed at the TV audiences and cameras so all could see and hear their vulgar behavior.

But the wrestling world would find out soon enough that the leader of DX, who was now known throughout the circuit as Triple H, was also one hell of a wrestler, who could win titles and clash with the big boys as well as anybody.

Since joining the World Wrestling Federation, Triple H has won four WWF World Championships, four Intercontinental straps, one tag-team title, two European Championships, and one King of the Ring (1997) tourney. He recently joined the short list of Grand Slam WWF champions, holding four major titles (World, Euro, Tag, and IC) at least once in his career.

He seems to be at his best when challenges are on the line. He won his first-ever WWF Pay-Per-View bout over Bob Holly in 1995 at SummerSlam in Pittsburgh. In 1997 he beat Ahmed Johnson and Mick Foley to become the King of the Ring. At SummerSlam '99 in Ames, Iowa, Triple H defeated Mankind to garner his first-ever WWF World Championship. His most recent WWF title came when he edged The Rock in a sixty-minute Iron Man match at Judgment Day on May 21, 2000, in Louisville, Kentucky, when he pinned "The People's Champ" six times to The Rock's five. His first and only tag-team title came on April 29, 2001, when Triple H and Steve Austin knocked off The Undertaker and Kane at Backlash '01 in Chicago's Allstate Arena.

In his illustrious career, Triple H, also known as "The Game," has kicked some serious ass without ever having to kiss any. He has feuded and battled with superstars like "Stone Cold" Steve Austin, The Rock, The Undertaker, Mankind, Kurt Angle, Chris Jericho, Kane, Chris Benoit, Vince McMahon, Owen Hart, Goldust, Marc Mero, Jeff Hardy, The Big Show, and countless others.

Another great thing about this wrestling megastar, which some may think unordinary for a superstar heel, is his willingness to put other lower-tier wrestlers over whenever possible. While losing or taking a beating from a lesser-known foe may not be good for "The Game's" career, he doesn't mind at all as long as he keeps generating heat from the audience for the federation.

You can't help but to love to hate this Game!

The Undertaker

November 2001 marked the eleven-year anniversary of The Undertaker's debut in the World Wrestling Federation. While the 6-foot-10 mammoth of a man has been mostly known for his Lord of Darkness persona around the wrestling circuit, nowadays he comes full force at his opponents with an attitude that has "American Bad Ass" written all over it.

His new personality first came on the scene on May 21, 2000, at a Judgment Day event in Louisville, Kentucky. The Undertaker, who had been out of action for nine months for health reasons, returned to the squared circle in stunning fashion, as he rode into Freedom Hall on his Harley-Davidson motorcycle during a Rock/Triple H match.

Without missing a beat, the well-rested grappler got off his hog and proceeded to lay the smackdown on the McMahon/Helmsley faction by chokeslamming a shocked Triple H during the final stages of an Iron Man match in front of the sold-out crowd. No longer did the wrestler possess his gothic warrior look—he now resembled a Hell's Angels biker, donning sunglasses and a bandanna to boot!

The 328-pound gladiator came on the WWF scene in November 1990 at the Survivor Series as a mystery partner to Ted DiBiase's "Million Dollar Team." He waltzed into the arena on that Thanksgiving night led by his first manager Brother Love and proceeded to knock in some heads on his first night in wrestling's top federation.

His first opponent ever on the WWF mat was KoKo B. Ware, who he wasted no time defeating by using his lethal Tombstone Piledriver. He then took on Dusty Rhodes, who he took out with his ever-dangerous chokeslam hold. Although he didn't go on to win the '90 Survivor Series, he proved that he was ready to rumble with anyone who got in his way.

The year 1991 proved to be big in the career of The 'Taker as he not only made his first-ever appearance at WrestleMania, he also had the chance to win his first-ever WWF Championship against none other than Hulk Hogan—the world's most popular wrestler!

The Hogan/Undertaker battle was anything but your typical good vs. evil rivalry. With Paul Bearer now at The Undertaker's side there was no telling what would happen when the two giants of wrestling squared off. Hulkamaniacs all over wondered if good was going to be conquered by evil every time these two squared off in the ring. At the 1991 Survivor Series, The Undertaker would show the entire wrestling world that he was for real, when he took on The Hulkster in a championship match billed as "The Gravest Challenge."

Hogan knew he was in trouble during the contest when he hit The Undertaker with the Big Boot and his powerful move didn't have any effect on his opponent. The Undertaker dominated Hulk Hogan in the main event match that night at Joe Louis Arena in Detroit, Michigan, also nailing him with a Tombstone to get him the pin and win in front of the stunned, sold-out crowd.

Even though his first title reign only lasted a week, as Hogan would win back his title on December 3, 1991, at a Tuesday in Texas match, the WWF newcomer sent a message to all his fellow grapplers. The entire WWF roster now knew that The Undertaker was capable of not just beating up his foes between the ropes, but also of winning championship gold from anyone who held the belt.

The following year, The Undertaker saw his character take a 360-degree turn with the fans. The dark gladiator went from being one of the most hated villains in the federation, to one of the most beloved wrestlers on the circuit. During 1992, The Undertaker waged memorable wars against his former ally Jake "The Snake" Roberts and also the Ugandan Giant, Kamala.

At WrestleMania VIII, The 'Taker took out Roberts in an awesome match that was highlighted by him Tombstoning "The Snake" on the steel floor outside the ring. The war between Kamala and the Lord of Darkness really came to a head at the '92 Survivor Series, when the two took part in the first-ever Casket match. The Undertaker and the Ugandan Giant traded several fierce blows in this tilt and it wasn't until The 'Taker nailed his huge opponent with a chokeslam followed by a blast from his trusty urn that he was able to down Kamala. The dark warrior then took his fallen foe and placed him in a coffin and nailed it shut, adding insult to injury.

In 1993 some thought The Undertaker met his match in a beast-of-a-man known as Giant Gonzalez. The two first met up at the 1993 Royal Rumble and would battle the whole year through. At the Rumble, The Undertaker seemed to be breezing along through the competition until Harvey Wippleman came through the curtain with an unscheduled grappler in the thirty-man tournament. Damien

Demento was scheduled to be the seventeenth man in the ring, but wisely kept off the mat and let the Giant through.

After that memorable night, wrestling fans all over knew who Giant Gonzalez was after he manhandled and laid out The Undertaker with a chokeslam at the Rumble. They would meet up again at WrestleMania and then again at SummerSlam, where The 'Taker rid the federation of Gonzalez's ugly mug in a "Rest in Peace" match. The RIP match was a no-holds-barred match that was set up to have no DQs and no countouts.

Even though Gonzalez was beating on him with a chair in the beginning of the match, The Undertaker defeated Giant Gonzalez in stunning fashion as he clotheslined his foe four times before going to the top rope and hitting him with a lethal clothesline to get the pin and extinguish the behemoth from the WWF.

In the years that followed, The Undertaker would become more powerful and lethal in the ring. Each new face that entered the federation knew that at some point, if they wanted to make a name for themselves, they would have to endure the wrath of the leader of the dark side.

One of the most challenging years in the career of The 'Taker was 1997, as he had to take on some of the best that the WWF had to offer almost on a nightly basis. Everyone that was anyone in the federation wanted a piece of him.

His best moment of that year came at WrestleMania 13, when he defeated Sycho Sid to win his second WWF title. In the weeks and months that followed, The Undertaker would take on the likes of Mankind, Steve Austin, Faarooq, and Vader, who all wanted to take his belt from him, but they would all fail.

He would eventually lose his strap to Bret "The Hitman" Hart at SummerSlam that year, but only due to the help of an illegal chair shot from the special referee for the evening, Shawn Michaels.

Michaels and The Undertaker would be involved in some memorable tussles from here on out, most notably the Hell in a Cell face-off, a match never before seen in the federation. The two wrestlers fought almost to the death for twenty minutes straight. The Undertaker bloodied "The Heartbreak Kid" to a pulp and just when it seemed as though Michaels would fall to his fearsome rival, a scary figure appeared on the scene and attacked The Phenom. The masked monster turned out to be none other than Kane, The Undertaker's long-lost brother. Kane then Tombstoned his own flesh and blood in front of Michaels, allowing him to limp away with the victory.

Kane would wreak havoc on his brother's career all the way up to March 29, 1998, when The Undertaker would finally square off against his brother at WrestleMania XIV. The crowd in Boston, Massachusetts, surely got their money's worth from this matchup. They not only got to watch a blood-brother feud firsthand, they also got to see Kane Tombstone baseball great Pete Rose into the mat.

The blow to Rose was a sign of things to come as Kane took the offensive early and often to his older brother. Kane was applying some pretty impressive offense to his relative, but just when it looked like The Big Red Machine was going to be victorious, the sleeping giant awoke.

'Taker eventually got the win over his younger sibling, but only after hitting the gruesome being with an assortment of maneuvers. On three separate occasions after hitting Kane with a Tombstone, The Undertaker tried for the win. His final flurry, which included a flying clothesline and another Tombstone, proved to be fatal, as UT finally got the victory.

Several months later, The Undertaker again defeated his brother. He teamed up with Steve Austin to defeat Kane and Mankind, winning the WWF Tag Team titles at Fully Loaded on July 26, 1998. UT would win another four tag titles over the years with partners such as The Big Show (2), The Rock, and his brother, Kane. He would also add another World title to his resume. At an Over the Edge event on May 23, 1999, in Kansas City, The Undertaker beat his former tag partner, "Stone Cold," in front of the Missouri crowd for his third WWF Championship.

During his prestigious career, The 'Taker has appeared in nine WrestleManias dating back to 1991 when he edged Jimmy "Super-Fly" Snuka at WrestleMania XII. Since then he has kept his unbeaten streak alive, defeating a pretty impressive list of ring kings like Jake "The Snake" Roberts (WrestleMania VII), Giant Gonzalez (Wrestle-Mania IX), King Kong Bundy (WrestleMania XI), Diesel (Wrestle-Mania XII), Sycho Sid (WrestleMania 13), Kane (WrestleMania XIV), the Big Boss Man (WrestleMania XV), and Triple H (Wrestle-Mania X7).

Not only has The Phenom fared well in these Super Bowls of wrestling, he has also risen to the occasion week in and week out whenever someone dared challenge his demon-hood. No matter who the foe, The Undertaker always seems to rise to the occasion. Over the years, he has gone toe-to-toe with wrestlers such as Hulk Hogan, "Stone Cold" Steve Austin, The Rock, Triple H, Bret "The Hitman" Hart, Mankind, Kurt Angle, Rikishi, Chris Jericho, Booker T, Diamond Dallas Page, and his monstrous brother, Kane.

One of his only regrets to date is that he never got a chance to wrestle one of the legends of the game, the late, great—and equally monstrous—Andre the Giant.

Rob Van Dam

R ob Van Dam is one of the most schooled and lethal wrestlers in the business today. The Michigan native not only learned to wrestle at eighteen years old from the Original Sheik, but he also added to his wrestling repertoire by studying martial arts, making him a double threat inside the ring. The athletic kid from Battle Creek learned Tae Kwon Do, karate, aikido, kendo, and kickboxing at two local dojos as a teenager from two very talented teachers, Kit Lykins and Terry Gay.

Before entering the wrestling world, Van Dam took what he learned in the dojos to the test when he tried his hand(s) (and feet) at professional kickboxing. In 1990, a strong man contest in Kalamazoo also caught his interest, so he entered and wound up finishing in second place. While the youngster was very talented, he quickly learned that there was very little money to be made in either sport.

Later in the year, Van Dam made his wrestling debut against his best friend at the time, Dango Nguyen, who was also a student of the Sheik. Nguyen and Van Dam enjoyed learning the ropes together from the legendary wrestler, but once the two buddies squared off against one another in a match in Toledo, Ohio, their friendship was never the same.

From there the rookie wrestler, then known as Rob Zakowski, took to the independent circuits in Michigan, Ohio, Tennessee, and Indiana looking not only to make a name for himself, but also to try and earn a living. One of the first places to give Zakowski a shot was the United States Wrestling Association (USWA) in Memphis, Tennessee. The young and eager grappler replaced Chris Candido in 1991 on the indie federation's tour and wound up squaring off against Sabu, the nephew of the Original Sheik, in his first match on the circuit.

After a two-month stint in the USWA, Zakowski hooked up with the South Atlantic Pro Wrestling promotion, where he clashed with Rikki Nelson over the Light-Heavyweight title, and also garnered the tag-team title with his partner Chaz Rocco on July 23, 1992, from the Ringlords (Dapper Dan and Speedy Gonzales).

Before joining forces with World Championship Wrestling in late 1992, the 6-foot, 227-pound warrior moved on to work for independents such as the International Championship Wrestling Alliance, Championship Wrestling Federation, Independent Wrestling Federation, and All Star Wrestling. While working in the ICWA in Florida he also worked as a bouncer to supplement his income, as he wasn't making enough money in the ring to pay the bills.

During his time on the Florida circuit, a local promoter by the name of Ron Slinker gave Zakowski the Rob Van Dam moniker that he uses on the mat to this very day. Slinker gave the young wrestler the ring name because of his resemblance to the action-movie star Jean-Claude Van Damme and also because of his kickboxing background.

Even though he was having trouble balancing his bills, Van Dam was having no trouble giving his foes their dues. The talented grappler gained immediate credibility when he won the IWF Television championship over Damien Stone.

Toward the end of '92, Van Dam was brought in to the WCW by Bill Watts and wrestled as Robbie V. The disappointed newcomer didn't stay too long in the federation, as there weren't too many wrestlers who wrestled the same hardcore style as he did. Even though he was getting way more TV exposure at this time because of the WCW's national TV audience, he wasn't satisfied because he was mainly a jobber in the federation at the time who was helping put other guys over. He tangled with grapplers such as Scotty Flamingo (Raven) and Shanghai Pierce (Mideon), while also helping out guys like Vinnie Vegas (Kevin Nash) come away with victories.

Instead of staying on as a lower-tier wrestler in the WCW, Van Dam took his act on the road and started wrestling overseas for All-Japan Pro Wrestling as well as in the States. In the next few years of his career, the hungry wrestler took on any and all during his time away from home, quickly turning himself into a well-oiled wrestling machine.

He not only competed in his first tour of international wrestling duty in Japan in 1993, but he would also take on and defeat Luscious Lonnie for the All-Star Wrestling title in Hazlehurst, Georgia, on March 26, 1994. Less than a year later, Van Dam would defeat Raven for the PSW Cordele City title. In October 1995 Van Dam scored an impressive victory overseas when he defeated Kentaro Shiga at All-Japan's twenty-third anniversary show in Tokyo.

Also in 1995, Van Dam took a big gamble and returned to the tag scene, where he teamed with Bobby Bradley wrestling for the National Wrestling Council in Las Vegas, Nevada. While in the NWC, the duo added another championship title to Van Dam's already extensive resume. He and Bradley teamed as the Aerial Assault and not only won the belts together, but also wreaked havoc on all the teams in the federation who dared to challenge them and their lethal finishing move, the Suicide Bomber.

In 1996, when Van Dam had just about had enough of rolling the dice in Vegas, his biggest career opportunity came knocking on the door in the form of Extreme Championship Wrestling, an association based in Philadelphia, Pennsylvania, at the urging of his friend and foe, Sabu.

In January, Van Dam made his ECW debut at House Party '96 and defeated Axl Rotten on the night's supercard, beginning a love affair with the ECW fans. A short while later Van Dam would also begin another ECW relationship, but this one was anything but lovely. After coming back from a two-month layoff due to a wrist injury, Van Dam would go toe-to-toe with the very man who got him his job at the federation, Sabu.

The two first squared off on April 20, 1996, at a Hostile City Showdown, which will not only go down in history as the first match between the two talented wrestlers, but also a match that showcased a memorable furniture wrecking aerial war between the two. No wrestler or piece of arena property was safe on that night.

After the highly entertaining match was over, Sabu, the already established ECW star, offered to shake the loser Van Dam's hand out of friendship and respect, but the baby face blew him off big time when he offered a hand in return, only to pull back just before their flesh met. As he turned to leave the ring, the ECW fans got all over their new star, as chants of "Assh*!$" filled the arena.

Thus, a new ECW heel was born!

The two would clash several more times throughout 1996, but

would make peace later in the year and take on the stiff tag competition that existed in the ECW. Their first matchup came in September 1996 at a Worlds Collide event, where Van Dam and Sabu took on Doug Furnas and Dan Kroffat. While the match ended in a thirty-minute draw, their foes and the rest of the tag circuit were put on alert as the duo looked lethal as a tandem.

Their next opponents were the Eliminators (Perry Saturn and John Kronus) at November to Remember, where the winning duo would get a shot at the tag title holders at the time, Da Gangstas (New Jack and Mustafa Saed). Again their match ended in a draw, forcing a three-way dance between the Eliminators, Da Gangstas, and Van Dam and Sabu for the title. The two again came away without a victory, as they were the first duo eliminated from the match, but not to worry, Sabu and Van Dam later went on to win two tag titles together on the ECW circuit.

In April 1997 ECW planned its first Pay-Per-View, Barely Legal, and to his surprise, Rob Van Dam was left off the card. Steamed that he was ignored for the PPV, Van Dam showed up at a rival's show in Savannah, Georgia, where several of his friends were wrestling for the WCW. While at the Nitro show, Van Dam not only talked about old times with his wrestling buddies, but he also got into a serious conversation with WCW head honcho, Eric Bischoff, who wanted to bring the ECW grappler on board.

While the offer was tempting to RVD at the time, he declined because he knew his loyalties still lay with the ECW. As a matter of fact, Van Dam did get to take part in the Barely Legal PPV when one of the participants, Chris Candido, went down with an injury and couldn't perform. Van Dam would not only take Candido's place on the card against Lance Storm, but he would also get the pin and win on this night, much to the crowd's displeasure. This PPV victory was also the start of an amazing unbeaten string for Van Dam, as he would soon earn the nickname "Mr. PPV" because of all the wins he piled on during these paid ECW events.

After beating Storm, Van Dam heard the loud chants of "You sold out" echoing in the arena. He responded to the crowd by giving them an earful, issuing a statement to all wrestling promoters stating that he was available to work Monday nights.

Keeping true to his words, Van Dam became the self-proclaimed "Mr. Monday Night" when he showed up on a WWF RAW Is War broadcast together with Jerry "The King" Lawler on May 12, 1997. He took on and defeated Jeff Hardy with his infamous move, the Split-Legged Moonsault, as part of a WWF/ECW angle.

The WWF/ECW angle would go on a little while longer but ultimately came to an end when the WWF wanted Van Dam to lose to the Road Dogg via a countout on a June 1997 RAW. Van Dam refused and walked out on the federation, thus becoming Mr. Ex–Monday Night.

After being suspended from the ECW for a month for his Monday Night antics, RVD returned to action in the ECW and picked up right where he left off. Less than a year later, on April 4, 1998, Van Dam won the ECW television title from the much bigger and stronger Bam Bam Bigelow in Buffalo, New York. Two months later he and Sabu captured their first tag-team title from Chris Candido and Lance Storm on June 6, 1998.

Van Dam held onto his TV title for almost two years—an ECW record—facing and beating everyone who got in his way. Among the grapplers who fell prey to RVD during this amazing title run were Skull Von Krush, Mikey Whipwreck, Doug Furnas, Ulf Hermann, Jerry Lynn, Lance Storm, Tommy Dreamer, Mike Lozansky, Balls Mahoney, Chris Candido, Rod Price, John Kronus, and many more.

When ECW folded in April 2001, Van Dam took some time

away from the ring to spend with his wife, Sonya, and also to give his body a rest. When he felt he was ready to go back to work, he hit the indies and Japan up for some ring work, eventually making his way back to one of the Big Two.

Van Dam made his official WWF debut on the July 9, 2001, edition of RAW, when the ECW Invasion took place in the federation. Longtime ECW owner, Paul Heyman, who was now making a living behind a WWF mic calling the action for the TV audience, stunned the wrestling world when he rallied up his former troops to try and overthrow the WWF.

A supposed handicap match that pitted Kane against Lance Storm and Mike Awesome really turned out to be Kane and Chris Jericho against the two former ECWers. Van Dam and Tommy Dreamer entered the ring and began helping Storm and Awesome. Then a whole slew of WWF wrestlers, like Tazz, the Dudley Boyz, Raven, and Rhyno came out and it looked like there was going to be an all-out war, but instead all the grapplers joined forces and beat on Kane and Jericho. Even though Kane and Jericho got the win by disqualification, Heyman's henchmen made a statement to all the fans and talent in attendance—the ECW was back and better than ever!

Wrestling fans were even more shocked when Shane McMahon, the new owner of the WCW, announced that the ECW and WCW were now merging their efforts to try and rid the world of his father's federation. The new WCW honcho also pointed out that this would be a joint family effort, as his sister, Stephanie McMahon-Helmsley, was now the new owner of the ECW.

Van Dam did his part to help the young McMahon owners. On July 22, RVD beat WWF superstar Jeff Hardy to win the WWF Hardcore title in Cleveland's Gund Arena. In less than three months the title changed hands five times with RVD coming away with three of them. Another impressive Hardcore win for Van Dam came on September 10 in San Antonio, Texas, when he beat another WWF fan favorite, Kurt Angle.

His most impressive victory to date came in a non-title match, when he pinned former WWF champion Steve Austin on September 4 during a SmackDown! taping in Toronto. Three weeks later, RVD also opened some eyes at Unforgiven when he successfully defended his Hardcore belt against another WWF monster of the mat, Chris Jericho, nailing the Lionheart with the Van Daminator and also a five-star frog splash for the pin. Less than a month later the most popular WWF personality, The Rock, wanted a piece of Van Dam and his Hardcore title, but the outcome was the same as the Jericho bout, with RVD coming away with more than just a piece of The Rock!

How to Become a Professional Wrestler

So you want to become a professional wrestler? Well, you might find out the hard way it is not as easy as you think. Having a dream and the desire to pursue it are only the first two steps . . . and the *easiest* steps on the road to becoming a professional bonebender. Those of you who have been watching the MTV series *WWF Tough Enough* know that it takes a lot of hard work, dedication, training, and aching muscles to succeed. But never take for granted the thousands of others who are trying to accomplish the same goal—the competition.

To be in the first season of *WWF Tough Enough*, for example, over 4,000 applicants sent in videotapes hoping to get the chance for a shot to compete in the World Wrestling Federation (WWF), *the* place to be for professional grapplers. It proved to be tough right from the beginning when only 230 of those thousands of applicants were actually invited for a tryout. Then, it only got *tougher.* By the next day those 230 were cut down to just 25! Do the math and you can easily see the chances of making it in wrestling's major league is even tougher than making it into Major League Baseball, the National Football League, the National Hockey League, or the National Basketball Association!

Sounds discouraging? Well, don't despair. There are other ways to carve out a career in the squared circle. It is certainly not as easy as picking out a catchy ring name and colorful outfit, but of those who have received the proper training, many have gone on to successful careers in the mat sport. Those who are not working in the spotlight of the WWF lead a less glamorous existence, for sure, but, nevertheless, are gainfully employed and doing what they love to do. As in any other profession, the proper training is required. You can watch an accountant add up numbers all day long that but that doesn't qualify you to sit down behind a desk and do the same. The same applies to wrestling. You can watch it all you want. You can be the sport's biggest fan, but you can't just step into the ring and expect to compete with the big boys. Like that aforementioned accountant who went to school to learn his trade, so must you.

Many men and women who decided to pursue their dreams of becoming wrestlers, managers, valets, and referees sought out professional instruction and are now working in the sport's independent promotions, often referred to as the minor leagues or "feeder federations"—such as Ohio Valley Wrestling (OVW) or the Heartland Wrestling Association (HWA)—hoping to get called up to the "bigs." Such is the case with *WWF Tough Enough* winners Maven and Nidia, who were each initially awarded one-year contracts to one of the feeder feds and hoped to someday make it to the ranks of the WWF.

A BRIEF HISTORY OF THE "SPORT OF KINGS"

To put things in perspective, a little history is necessary. If you are wondering which came first, wrestling or wrestling instruction, consider that the oldest sport in the world is running, and the second-oldest sport is wrestling. Assuming that our ancestors grappled with each other long before they spoke sensible syllables, the names for moves came later, as did formal training for "the sport of kings."

It is well known that the Greeks and Romans wrestled for sport in their public and private gymnasiums and as social entertainment. In Japan, the art of sumo was revered and its athletes celebrated. North American Indians made grappling a popular activity among their tribes. England offered wrestling as amusement and eventually carried it to America in carnival form, where it began to catch on.

It has been documented in history books that Abraham Lincoln wrestled in a round circle, or "ring" drawn in the dirt, for sport—and also for a few pennies—before he was elected president. And, as we all know, his likeness eventually even wound up gracing the coins! As the sport gained momentum in the States, names such as Lewis, Gotch, and Londos represented the "halcyon days" of wrestling as a true sport; matches could last hours before one man wore the other down and got the win. Today, it is unusual for a wrestling match to last more than five minutes, so accustomed we have become to "fast-food entertainment."

In those days, a grizzly, veteran grappler might take on an apprentice or protégé, training him over a period of several years, and eventually breaking him into the business when he was deemed "ready," much as a carpenter or blacksmith would train an apprentice at that time. Today, the prime source of wrestling training comes from wrestling schools, which undertake to instruct aspiring wrestlers in the basics, hone their skills, and get them ready for their first professional match.

THE ADVENT OF WRESTLING SCHOOLS

All wrestling schools are not created equal, and many come and go. But Slammers Wrestling Gym opened in 1989 and is still going strong. In fact, Slammers originally opened not as a school but as a place where any wrestler, whether pro or wanna-be, could walk in the door, pay a fee and, after signing a liability release, utilize an authentic professional wrestling ring. A few teachers brought students, but most who came to Slammers just wanted to get in the ring and pretend to be their favorite wrestlers, bouncing off the ropes and delivering leg drops a la Hulk Hogan. It was a lot of fun for a lot of folks, but Slammers founder Verne Langdon saw that there were a lot of people out there who were serious about the sport and he set out to meet their needs.

First, he assembled a complete wrestling museum at Slammers, so that anyone coming to use the facility might be enlightened to the sport's rich history. Everything from legendary women's champ the Fabulous Moolah's diamond-encrusted eyeglasses to the entire wardrobe and personal effects of the one-and-only Gorgeous George (nee George Wagner) was displayed for all of the world to see. Huge vintage posters and photo enlargements by famed photographer Shirlie Montgomery hung from the walls while giant mirrors were mounted so that the wrestlers could see how they looked "in action." Theatrical stage and television lighting illuminated the ring where wrestling hopefuls came to practice.

It wasn't long before professional instruction was added and visitors came to see this one-of-a-kind place, a kind of "field of dreams for grunt 'n' groaners." After their experiences at Slammers, some of these visitors then returned home and attempted to create their own versions of Slammers. Soon Roland Alexander's All Pro Wrestling School, Al Snow's Bodyslammers Wrestling Gym, and Terry Funk's Funk U were up and running. Now in its twelfth year, Slammers continues its well-structured, no-nonsense professional training (with emphasis on the word *professional*), under the dedicated tutelage of Head Slammer El Toro Bravo, himself an original product of the world's premier wrestling university (Slam U), museum, and gym. In fact, Slammers is referred to by many in the profession as "America's #1 Wrestling School."

"Slammers wrestlers have earned a reputation in the sport for really turning up the heat, not pulling any punches, and giving the fans real wrestling matches," explains El Toro Bravo. "When we 'get down,' the rest get out!

"Well, too bad, so sad, bye-bye! Slammers isn't for crybabies. It's for wrestlers who like to hurt and be hurt, wrestlers who like to mix it up, and most importantly: wrestlers who love to wrestle!" the Head Slammer warns.

"Slammers was built on that concept from the first day we opened and nothing has changed. We still love to wrestle and expect *you* to share the same passion. Any less and *we don't want you!* Slammers wrestling is not a 'sometime' thing here for you when you are bored with life or between girlfriends," warns El Toro Bravo. "If you don't want to *do* it to death, don't come to Slammers. We're into it and you'd better be too!"

THE CURRICULUM

Sounds tough! Still interested in becoming a pro? OK, let's get down to the nitty-gritty—the curriculum. Here's a closer look at Slam U, from which 98 percent of its graduates are wrestling professionally for independent promoters.

As is the case with most wrestling schools, applicants are first required to come in for a sit-down interview to discuss what it is they are looking to accomplish as far as wrestling is concerned. This, of course, is necessary in order to eliminate the "wanna-bes" from the wrestlers. Students have to prove that they are willing to make all the sacrifices that are involved in wrestling. Unsuitable applicants will be turned away with a suggestion of another profession that is more suitable for them. Instructors certainly don't want to waste their time with students who are less than serious. Prospective students, on the other hand, shouldn't waste their own time—and money—unless they are absolutely sure pro wrestling is the only life for them.

If the applicant passes the interview, the next phase is the actual "in-ring" interview. This varies with each new hopeful. Some may work in the ring for one to six weeks in this phase while others can pass this portion in just one session. The purpose is to see how athletic and physically fit the student is. Be forewarned, this part of the training can sometimes get ugly. Students have been known to quit in tears, their bodies in shock from being slammed on the unforgiving ring surface. When confident students are reduced to quivering wrecks that is when the realities—and *pain*—of pro wrestling are driven home. This is also where the wheat is separated from the chaff, to use an old cliché.

Once the student passes this stage, school is officially "in session." At Slam U, classes are held every Sunday of each month, for two hours. The importance of attending each and every class is emphasized, as one week can consist of instruction on body slams and arm bars and the next on ring psychology. Slammers doesn't adhere to a strict curriculum. This is to prevent students from learning wrestling holds and maneuvers the wrong way. Rather, Slammers teaches not only the mechanics of the moves but takes pride in their proper application as well. You don't go on to the next move until you get "this one" right.

Constant grappling and offensive wrestling are part of each session. Once a move is learned it is practiced and applied. Ring psychology is of the utmost importance at Slammers and is stressed at each and every lesson. In fact, one of the "Golden Rules" of Slammers is "Less Is More," meaning quality over quantity.

"Our students—because we hand-pick them—are voraciously enthusiastic and readily adaptable (for the most part) to the high intensity level of the classes," says El Toro Bravo.

Once a student can grasp this philosophy and the teaching staff is satisfied with the student's progress, he/she can then participate in the monthly wrestling shows held at Slammers. This is an opportunity for the students to apply all that they have learned into a live wrestling exhibition, in front of an audience that consists of family, friends, fellow wrestlers, and others. Upon completion of all classes and the passing of a final exam, the student is deemed a Slammers Wrestling Gym, Slam U Graduate.

This particular training regimen is a two-year course. The length and some other aspects will vary with each individual wrestling school, but most of the schools out there today are modeled on Slammers.

PAY YOUR DUES

Slam U graduates begin active competition in the Slammers Wrestling Federation (SWF). Theatrics are an integral part of the course and once the mechanics of the sport are mastered, budding wrestlers hone their theatrical skills in SWF matches. Every wrestling match tells a story and wrestlers have to play to the crowd while trading moves with an opponent.

With each match, wrestlers gain experience, learning what makes the crowd "pop" and what makes them groan. Each match has a beginning, a middle, and an end. The more complete a wrestler's background in his sport, the better that wrestler will be at entertaining his audience.

Many schools, like Slammers, are affiliated with independent wrestling promotions that act as launching pads for their graduates. Schools that don't have such affiliations are often able to recommend graduates to independent promotions in the area and provide the proper contacts. The rest is up to you.

After each wrestler's pro debut it is up to them to move onward and upward, seeking bigger audiences and more television exposure in different promotions, moving on from regional promotions to getting national exposure. It isn't easy, by any means, but with the proper training, you've got a fighting chance!

THE NEXT STEP

Still think you have what it takes to make it as a pro? Think you are the next "Stone Cold" Steve Austin? The next incarnation of The Rock? Then contact Slammers Wrestling Gym at (818) 897-6603 or check out the website www.slammers.com for more information.

TEN OTHER TOP WRESTLING SCHOOLS

If you are not from the Southern California area and are unable to relocate to study at Slam U, here are some particulars about some other well-respected wrestling schools across the country that may be more convenient for you to attend.

The Monster Factory

This wrestling school is run by former WWF wrestler "Pretty Boy" Larry Sharpe, who has been called a "worldly scholar with impeccable academic credentials. A professor who demands the very best from his students" by *Evening* magazine.

The Monster Factory has two locations, one in southern New Jersey and the other in Washington, D.C. Some of its more accomplished graduates are King Kong Bundy, The Big Show, the Godfather, D'Lo Brown, Chaz, Raven, Chris Candido, and Tammy Lynn Sytch. Bundy, in fact, calls The Monster Factory "the postgraduate school of professional wrestling."

Check out the website at www.monsterfactory.com for a look at the training regimen. You can also write or call The Monster Factory at either of its two locations:

The Monster Factory
P.O. Box 345
Westville, NJ 08093
(856) 456-5000

The Monster Factory
6519 Chillum Place
Washington, D.C.
(202) 966-1111

The Wild Samoan Training Center

The Wild Samoan Training Center is the only professional wrestling training center endorsed by the World Wrestling Federation, which says a lot. The head trainer is Afa the Wild Samoan, a former WWF World Tag Team champion who has been training pros for over twenty-five years.

This school offers instruction on becoming a professional wrestler, manager, or referee. Some of its more famous graduates include Yokozuna, Junkyard Dog, Doink The Clown, Hulk Hogan, Paul Orndorff, Michael Hayes, Luna Vachon, Kanyon, and Billy Kidman, among others. What's more, The Wild Samoan Training Center has two locations in Pennsylvania and one in Florida and is planning to expand internationally.

Check out The Wild Samoan Training Center on the web at www.WildSamoan.com or call (610) 435-0251. You can also write to:

The Wild Samoan Training Center
P.O. Box 251
Whitehall, PA 18052-0251

Killer Kowalski Institute of Professional Wrestling

This school, located in the Boston, Massachusetts, area, is run by wrestling legend Killer Kowalski, a former bad guy who has turned over a new leaf and is now training the superstars of the future. Inducted into the WWF's Hall of Fame in 1996, Kowalski certainly has the required credentials. Some of his recent graduates who have been making noise on the professional wrestling scene are Chyna, Triple H, Saturn, Albert, and Killer Kowalski, Jr.

For more information, log on to the website at www.angelfire. com/wrestling/kowalskischool/ or write to:

Killer Kowalski Institute of Professional Wrestling
P.O. Box 67
Reading, MA 01867

You can also e-mail them at kowalskischool@aol.com.

Les Thatcher's Main Event Pro Wrestling Camp

Les Thatcher, who wrestled professionally from 1960–1979 and has been involved in the sport for over thirty-nine years, has been training wrestlers-to-be for over six years now. In addition to running the training camp, Thatcher also is the promoter for the Heartland Wrestling Association (HWA), one of the better-known feeder federations. He takes a hands-on approach and seeks students with desire, talent, and love of the sport. Thatcher and his trainees have been featured on MTV's *True Life: I Am a Professional Wrestler* and on ABC's *20/20* news show.

Check out the website at www.hwaonline.com/trainingcamp.html. For more information, call (513) 771-1650 or write to:

Les Thatcher's Main Event Pro Wrestling Camp
1220 Hillsmith Drive, Suite K
Cincinnati, OH 45215

Harley Race Wrestling Academy

Located in the "Show Me" state, this school is run by eight-time National Wrestling Alliance (NWA) World champion Harley Race, and he's ready to show you how to make it in the rough and tumble pro wrestling ranks. Candidates undergo a lengthy tryout program and those successful enough are then invited to join an extensive training program at the academy. Race also promotes World League Wrestling (WLW) cards and when their training is completed, wrestlers are required to license with the Missouri State Athletic Commission and are given the opportunity to wrestle in WLW.

Check out the website at www.harleyrace.com/wlw/hracademy. htm. For more information, call (573) 392-4100 or write to:

Harley Race Wrestling Academy
119 South Maple Street
Eldon, MO 65026

All Pro Wrestling Boot Camp

Roland Alexander's All Pro Wrestling (APW) Boot Camp was founded in 1991 and aspires to give students the valuable experience necessary along with the exposure they need to develop into main event talent. Alexander learned from some of the best, including legendary promoter Roy Shires and Hall of Fame wrestler Ray Stevens. He also promotes All Pro Wrestling cards, so graduates get the opportunity to debut at APW events.

Check out the website at www.allprowrestling.com/corporate/ aboutapw.htm. For more information, call (510) 785-8396 or write to:

All Pro Wrestling
21063 Cabot Blvd., Suite #1
Hayward, CA 94545

Skull Krushers Wrestling School

Skull Krushers Wrestling School is run by one of the sport's most flamboyant characters—"Exotic" Adrian Street. In addition to his accomplishments in the squared circle (he was a "champion throughout all continents"), Street has also had success as a painter and writer. In tandem with his valet, Miss Linda, they offer training for aspiring wrestlers, managers, valets, and referees. They also manufacture their own line of wrestling gear.

Check out the website at www.bizarebazzar.dotstar.net/school. htm. For more information, call (904) 934-8435 or write to:

Skull Krushers Wrestling School
P.O. Box 6188
Gulf Breeze, FL 32561

The Funking Conservatory

The Funking Conservatory is run by former NWA World champ Dory Funk, Jr., who until recently was the top trainer of WWF and earned the nickname "Coach" for instructing such top WWF superstars as Edge, Christian, Rhyno, Rikishi, and the Hardy Boyz. Funk also produces the weekly television show *!BANG!* and students at the conservatory will learn to wrestle and also be on television!

Check out the website at www.dory-funk.com You can also e-mail Dory at fuanku@dory-funk.com. For more information, call (352) 895-4658 or write to:

The Funking Conservatory
P.O. Box 771-702
Ocala, FL 34477-1702

Boogie's Wrestling Camp

Former wrestler Jimmy Valiant, otherwise known as "The Boogie Woogie Man," offers training sessions every Sunday afternoon from 12:00 noon until 4:00 P.M. The sessions are open to all, with no size or weight requirements for men and women. Valiant was a champion both on the singles and tag-team circuits and is eager to impart the knowledge he's acquired after over three decades of active wrestling in the ring.

Check out the website at www.jimmyvaliant.com/campd.htm. For more information, write to:

Boogie's Wrestling Camp
2916 Allegheny Springs Rd.
Shawsville, VA 24162

Windy City Pro Wrestling School

This Chicago-based school offers up to three rings for unlimited training, a complete weight training facility, videotaping equipment, and a flexible payment plan. Best of all, once your initial training is complete, you are guaranteed booking and television exposure!

Check out the website at www.windycityprowrestling.com. For more information, call (733) 978-7317 or (312) 719-7198. Or write to:

Windy City Wrestling Promotions, Inc.
P.O. Box 170048
Chicago, IL 60717

The Real Deal

1. ALBERT .... Matt Bloom

2. "STONE COLD" STEVE AUSTIN .... Steve Williams

3. CHRIS BENOIT .... Chris Benoit

4. THE BIG SHOW .... Paul Wight

5. BOOKER T .... Booker Huffman

6. CHRISTIAN .... Jason Reso

7. DEBRA .... Debra Williams

8. D-VON DUDLEY .... Devon Hughes

9. BUBBA RAY DUDLEY .... Mark Lomonica

10. **SPIKE DUDLEY** . . . . *Matthew Hyson*

11. **EDGE** . . . . *Adam Copeland*

12. **RIC FLAIR** . . . . *Richard Morgan Fliehr*

13. **MICK FOLEY** . . . . *Michael Francis Foley*

14. **JEFF HARDY** . . . . *Jeff Hardy*

15. **MATT HARDY** . . . . *Matt Hardy*

16. **HULK HOGAN** . . . . *Terry Bollea*

17. **CHRIS JERICHO** . . . . *Chris Irvine*

18. **KANE** . . . . *Glen Jacobs*

19. **LITA** . . . . *Amy Dumas*

20. **LINDA MCMAHON** . . . . *Linda McMahon*

21. **SHANE MCMAHON** . . . . *Shane McMahon*

22. **STEPHANIE MCMAHON** . . . . *Stephanie McMahon*

23. **VINCE MCMAHON** . . . . *Vince McMahon, Jr.*

24. **RAVEN** . . . . *Scott Levy*

25. **WILLIAM REGAL** . . . . *Darren Matthews*

26. **RHYNO** . . . . *Terry Gerin*

27. **STEVE RICHARDS** . . . . *Michael Manna*

28. **RIKISHI** . . . . *Solofa Fatu*

29. **THE ROCK** . . . . *Dwayne Johnson*

30. **SATURN** . . . . *Perry Satullo*

31. **AL SNOW** .... *Allen Sarven*

32. **LANCE STORM** .... *Lance Evers*

33. **TAJIRI** .... *Yoshihiro Tajiri*

34. **TAZZ** .... *Pete Senerca*

35. **TEST** .... *Andrew Martin*

36. **TRIPLE H** .... *Paul Levesque*

37. **TRISH STRATUS** .... *Trish Stratigias*

38. **THE UNDERTAKER** .... *Mark Calloway*

39. **ROB VAN DAM** .... *Rob Szakowski*

40. **X-PAC** .... *Sean Waltman*

The History of
WrestleMania

Every sport has its premier event. In baseball, it is the World Series, a tradition since 1903. In football, fans wait in anticipation
all season long for the annual Super Bowl, the clash of the NFL's top
two squads to determine who is number one. The Kentucky Derby is
without a doubt the event of the year in horse racing circles, with the
winner receiving acclaim across the globe. In ice hockey, the Stanley
Cup Finals showcase the sport's two best teams to establish who is
number one at the end of each season. Professional wrestling, you
will see, is no exception to the rule. Each year, mat fans look forward
to their sport's gala event, when the best of the best get to shine in

the spotlight as they climb into the squared circle to compete at WrestleMania, the most prestigious card in the sport!

Started by the World Wrestling Federation in 1985, the annual WrestleMania extravaganzas are the most watched of the promotion's many yearly events, attracting celebrities as well as wrestling's elite competitors. It is, in effect, the Super Bowl of the squared circle, the one day that defines the sport. And while it is a given that when spring is in the air, WrestleMania is not far behind, much has changed in regard to this star-studded spectacular over the years. Here's a look at Wrestle-Manias over the years and how each has earned its place in history.

WRESTLEMANIA I, MARCH 31, 1985, MADISON SQUARE GARDEN, NEW YORK, NY

The grand-daddy of them all took place in the World's Most Famous Arena and was the most successful event in the WWF's history, guaranteeing its status as a yearly event. Taking a cue from boxing, the WWF broadcast the event via the then-popular closed-circuit TV format and attracted over a million viewers, heady numbers for the time. It also attracted a host of non-wrestling celebrities, including the boxing legend Muhammad Ali; the late, great Yankee manager Billy Martin; the ultimate entertainer, Liberace; and Mr. T from the popular television series *The A-Team*.

The card itself featured the absolute top names in the sport at the time, including perhaps the most well-known wrestler of all time, Hulk Hogan! The Hulkster, the WWF World Champion, had been feuding with "Rowdy" Roddy Piper and had enlisted the help of his friend Mr. T to take on Piper and his crony "Mr. Wonderful" Paul Orndorff in a main-event tag-team match, making the very first WrestleMania ever one for the record books. But that's not all. Making this match even more significant was the involvement of Jimmy "Superfly" Snuka, one of the most popular wrestlers of the time, who accompanied Hogan and Mr. T to the ring, and "Cowboy" Bob Orton, who seconded the team of Piper and Orndorff.

The matchup was a wrestling fan's dream come true and it did not disappoint as the action was fast and furious, with all six men getting involved while the crowd cheered for the "good guys," represented by Hogan and his crew. The end came when Orton inadvertently hit Orndorff with the plaster cast on his arm, sending "Mr. Wonderful" crashing to the canvas where Hogan covered him for the pin and victory for his team! The crowd went wild and was rewarded with an extra treat when Piper and Orton blamed the loss on Orndorff and attacked him to provide some unexpected action! This set the stage for Orndorff's turn to becoming a fan favorite and figuring prominently in the WWF for the next few years to come.

Fans worldwide got their money's worth with the main event alone, but there was plenty more excitement on the talent-laden card, including a Women's Championship match that saw popular Wendi Richter, who was managed by pop star Cyndi Lauper, win the title from Leilani Kai. In addition, there was another title match, with the team of Nikolai Volkoff and The Iron Sheik defeating Mike Rotundo and Barry Windham for the WWF Tag Team Championship. And don't forget Andre the Giant's victory over Big John Studd in a Body Slam match!

Other matches at the first-ever WrestleMania were:

David Sammartino vs. Brutus Beefcake, Double DQ

Tito Santana defeated the Executioner

Junkyard Dog beat Greg Valentine, Countout

Ricky Steamboat defeated Matt Borne

King Kong Bundy won over S. D. Jones

WrestleMania I trivia: Which performer began his iron-man streak at this event, becoming the only person to appear at all seventeen WrestleManias? Answer: Ring Announcer Howard Finkel.

WRESTLEMANIA II, APRIL 7, 1986, NASSAU COLISEUM (NY), ROSEMONT HORIZON (CHICAGO, IL), AND LOS ANGELES SPORTS ARENA (CA)

The WWF managed to top itself with its second WrestleMania extravaganza, lining up the key talent in the sport along with another contingent of non-wrestling celebrities for its now-yearly spectacular. The big difference this year, however, was that the event took place in three separate arenas, making it the first of its kind in any sport! It was also the first WrestleMania to be broadcast via Pay-Per-View television.

From the start, WrestleMania II was unique with soul legend Ray Charles belting out his rendition of "America the Beautiful." Comedienne Joan Rivers served as special guest ring announcer and actress Susan St. James (*Kate & Allie*) served as a commentator alongside Vince McMahon. Hulk Hogan participated in the main event, this time taking on King Kong Bundy in a steel cage match! Hogan was iffy about the match, having suffered injured ribs at the hands of Bundy a few weeks earlier. He ignored doctors' warnings to not only compete, but beat his beefy challenger to retain his title, finishing off his foe with his famous leg drop!

Back again too were Roddy Piper and Mr. T, although not as

wrestlers. This time they faced each other in a special boxing match, which featured musician extraordinaire Cab Calloway and basketball great Darryl Dawkins as special guest judges. In Piper's corner was legendary boxing trainer Lou Duva but Mr. T proved to be the better boxer from the start. In fact, the Rowdy One got so frustrated that he completely forgot the rules and *body-slammed* Mr. T, getting disqualified and giving T the win!

The other ground-breaking match was a 20-Man Battle Royal, featuring a lineup of WWF superstars, including Bruno Sammartino, Pedro Morales, and Big John Studd *and* football greats such as Jimbo Covert, William "Refrigerator" Perry, Bill Fralic, Harvey Martin, Russ Francis, and Ernie Holmes. When all was said and done, it was the biggest of them all, Andre the Giant, who emerged victorious!

Other matches at WrestleMania II were:

Paul Orndorff vs. Don Muraco, Double Countout

Hoss Funk and Terry Funk defeated Junkyard Dog and Tito Santana

Randy "Macho Man" Savage pinned George "The Animal" Steele

Adrian Adonis pinned Uncle Elmer

Jake "The Snake" Roberts pinned George Wells

Ricky Steamboat pinned Hercules

Women's Champion the Fabulous Moolah defeated Velvet McIntyre

The British Bulldogs defeated Greg Valentine and Brutus Beefcake for the Tag Team Championship

Cpl. Kirschner beat Nikolai Volkoff via pinfall

WrestleMania II trivia: The Hogan vs. Bundy bout is the only cage match in WrestleMania history.

WRESTLEMANIA III, MARCH 29, 1987, PONTIAC SILVERDOME, PONTIAC, MI

Not content to rest on its laurels, the WWF reserved the Pontiac Silverdome for WrestleMania III, selling out the huge arena to pack in 93,173 fans, a record for an indoor sporting event. The reason? The main event pitted Hulk Hogan, who was in the third year of his WWF World Championship reign, against the Eighth Wonder of the World, Andre the Giant, the 7-foot-4, 520-pound behemoth who had turned against Hogan, his former ally, for a shot at the title.

Aretha Franklin got the spectators in the mood by singing "America the Beautiful" and celebrities Mary Hart of *Entertainment Tonight* fame and former baseball player and celebrity Bob Uecker served as roaming reporters, with Uecker also adding commentary throughout the card.

The noise was deafening as the blond bomber and Andre squared off, with the Giant taking the early advantage and almost ending the match in the first two minutes as Hogan attempted to body-slam the big man and failed. Yet, Hogan persevered and Hulkamania prevailed. The Hulkster astounded the crowd and those watching on Pay-Per-View as he successfully slammed the Giant, followed with his now-famous leg drop, and pinned Andre to retain his title!

Other highlights of this record-setting event were Ricky Steamboat beating "Macho Man" Randy Savage for the Intercontinental title, a match many consider to be one of the best ever in WrestleMania history, Jake "The Snake" Roberts having rock musician Alice Cooper in his corner as he went down in defeat at the hands of the Honky Tonk Man, and a mixed tag-team match featuring Hillbilly Jim and two midgets—Haiti Kid and Little Beaver—defeating King Kong Bundy and two midgets—Little Tokyo and Lord Little-brook.

Other matches at WrestleMania III were:

Roddy Piper defeated Adrian Adonis

The Iron Sheik and Nikolai Volkoff beat the Killer Bees, DQ

Rick Martel and Tom Zenk defeated Bob Orton and Don Muraco

Butch Reed pinned Koko B. Ware

Billy Jack Haynes vs. Hercules, Double Countout

The Hart Foundation and Danny Davis defeated the British Bulldogs and Tito Santana via pinfall

Harley Race pinned Junkyard Dog

Greg Valentine and Brutus Beefcake beat the Rougeau Brothers via pinfall

WrestleMania III trivia: Even though Roddy Piper's match at WrestleMania III was billed as his retirement match, "the Rowdy One" continued to compete for over a decade.

WRESTLEMANIA IV, MARCH 27, 1988, TRUMP PLAZA, ATLANTIC CITY, NJ

"What the World Is Watching" was the catchphrase for the WWF's gala event this year as millions watched via Pay-Per-View and closed-circuit television. It was another star-studded spectacular, featuring Gladys Knight singing "America the Beautiful," Vanna White of *Wheel of Fortune* fame in the backstage area, Bob Uecker as a roving reporter, and mogul Donald Trump and ex-boxing champ Sugar Ray Leonard at ringside.

For the first time ever, there was no WWF Champion coming into the event so WrestleMania IV presented an elimination tournament to crown a new champ. The tournament featured the biggest names in the business, including Hulk Hogan, Randy Savage, Andre the Giant, Ted DiBiase, Ricky Steamboat, Rick Rude, Jake Roberts, Don Muraco, Bam Bam Bigelow, One Man Gang, Greg Valentine, Dino Bravo, "Hacksaw" Jim Duggan, and Butch Reed. In the end, it was Savage and DiBiase battling for the Federation's top honor and it was the Macho Man who emerged victorious and was crowned the new champ!

Also on the WrestleMania IV card were:

A 20-man Battle Royal, won by Bad News Brown

Brutus Beefcake beat Honky Tonk Man, DQ

The Islanders and Bobby Heenan defeated the British Bulldogs and Koko B. Ware via pinfall

Demolition beat Strike Force for the Tag Team title

WrestleMania IV trivia: Going into WrestleMania IV the WWF Championship was declared vacant, the first time the title had ever been vacant since Buddy Rogers became the first WWF champion in 1962.

WRESTLEMANIA V, APRIL 2, 1989, TRUMP PLAZA, ATLANTIC CITY, NJ

Trump Plaza was again the setting for WrestleMania and, if possible, was an even better event than the previous year with a record-setting fourteen matches. Celebrities in the house included rap stars Run DMC, loudmouth talk-show host Morton Downey, Jr., and Donald Trump.

The highlight of the event was the birth of Hulkamania, as Hulk Hogan squared off against his former ally Randy Savage, the reigning WWF Champion, in the main event. The Macho Man had split from Hogan when he felt the Hulkster was paying too much attention to Savage's valet, Miss Elizabeth. Their WrestleMania V battle was a classic, with Savage gamely defending his title, but with his Hulkamaniacs cheering him on, the Hulkster prevailed and sent the Macho Man down to defeat, capturing the WWF World title for the second time!

Other matches at WrestleMania V were:

The Twin Towers defeated the Rockers by pinfall

The Red Rooster pinned Bobby Heenan

Ted DiBiase vs. Brutus Beefcake, Double Countout

Bad News Brown vs. Jim Duggan, Double DQ

The Bushwhackers beat the Rougeau Brothers via pinfall

Rick Rude won the Intercontinental Championship from the Ultimate Warrior

Mr. Perfect pinned the Blue Blazer

The Hart Foundation defeated Greg Valentine and Honky Tonk Man by pinfall

Hercules defeated King Haku

The Brain Busters defeated Strike Force via pinfall

Jake Roberts beat Andre the Giant, DQ

Dino Bravo defeated Ron Garvin

Demolition defeated the Powers of Pain and Mr. Fuji by pinfall

WrestleMania V trivia: Morton Downey, Jr., was a guest on a special Piper's Pit segment at WrestleMania V.

WRESTLEMANIA VI, APRIL 1, 1990, SKYDOME, TORONTO, ONTARIO

With WrestleMania VI, WrestleMania truly became an international event, as it was the first time the prestigious wrestling card was held outside of the United States. Additionally, it set a SkyDome attendance record with 67,678 fans in attendance, including actress Mary Tyler Moore. Other celebrities on hand were Rona Barrett, who interviewed Miss Elizabeth; Robert Goulet, who started things off by singing "O Canada;" and Steve Allen, who accompanied the Bolsheviks on the Russian national anthem.

But the center of attention was the main event, pitting the WWF's two biggest stars—and titles—on the line as WWF Champ Hulk Hogan and Intercontinental Champ the Ultimate Warrior squared off in the "Ultimate Challenge." It was a nip-and-tuck battle and just as it seemed that the Hulkster would prevail with his famous leg drop, the Warrior moved and pinned the stunned Hogan to capture both titles!

The other matches at WrestleMania VI were:

Rick Rude pinned Jimmy Snuka

Rick Martel defeated Koko B. Ware, Submission

The Big Boss Man pinned Akeem

Demolition defeated the Colossal Connection for the Tag Team Championship

Ted DiBiase beat Jake Roberts

Brutus Beefcake pinned Mr. Perfect

Jim Duggan pinned Dino Bravo

Roddy Piper vs. Bad News Brown, Double Countout

The Orient Express defeated the Rockers, Countout

The Hart Foundation beat the Bolsheviks via pinfall

Dusty Rhodes and Sapphire defeated Randy Savage and Sherri via pinfall

Barbarian pinned Tito Santana

WrestleMania VI trivia: Ten years before he would capture the WWF Tag Team titles with Christian, Edge sat ringside at WrestleMania VI wearing a "Hulk Rules!" T-shirt.

WRESTLEMANIA VII, MARCH 24, 1991, L.A. ARENA, LOS ANGELES, CA

With the Gulf War raging, WrestleMania VII took patriotism to new heights as, in the main event, fan favorite Hulk Hogan took on Iraqi sympathizer Sgt. Slaughter. On hand to witness the Hulkster's red, white, and blue victory were country star Willie Nelson, who opened the show with his rendition of "America the Beautiful;" TV host Regis Philbin, who provided commentary during the main event; Alex Trebek of *Jeopardy* fame, who served as guest ring announcer for the main event and also conducted some backstage interviews;

George Steinbrenner and Paul Maguire, who debated the use of instant replay in the WWF; and Marla Maples, who was guest timekeeper for the main event. There were plenty of celebrities at ringside too, including movie star Macaulay Culkin, billionaire Donald Trump, muscleman Lou Ferrigno, action-adventure star Chuck Norris, and *Happy Days* star Henry "The Fonz" Winkler.

Other matches at WrestleMania VII were:

The Rockers defeated the Barbarian and Haku via pinfall

Texas Tornado pinned Dino Bravo

Jake Roberts beat Rick "The Model" Martel in a blindfold match

The British Bulldog pinned the Warlord

The Nasty Boys defeated the Hart Foundation for the Tag Team Championship

The Mountie pinned Tito Santana

The Ultimate Warrior defeated Randy Savage in a retirement match

Virgil beat Ted DiBiase, Countout

Genichiro and Koji Kiao defeated Demolition via pinfall

Legion of Doom beat Power and Glory via pinfall

The Big Boss Man defeated Mr. Perfect, DQ

Earthquake pinned Greg Valentine

WrestleMania VII trivia: WrestleMania VII was originally scheduled to take place at the L.A. Coliseum, which seats over 100,000, but due to security concerns related to the Gulf War, the event was moved to the L.A. Arena.

WRESTLEMANIA VIII, APRIL 5, 1992, HOOSIER DOME, INDIANAPOLIS, IN

Over 60,000 fans packed the Hoosier Dome for a WrestleMania that boasted a double main event—the first pitting Randy Savage against "Nature Boy" Ric Flair, and the other featuring Hulk Hogan in what many thought would be the last match of his career. Celebrities on hand included Reba McIntyre, who sang "America the Beautiful," and *Family Feud* host Ray Combs, who made some of the ring introductions.

Savage was challenging Flair for the World title and had an even greater incentive than capturing the title belt—jealousy, for Flair had eyes for Savage's valet, Miss Elizabeth. Flair, known as the "dirtiest player in the game," pushed the Macho Man to the limit but the power of love gave Randy the inspiration to persevere and win the coveted championship for the second time.

In the second main event, Hogan faced Psycho Sid in a grudge match that was billed as the Hulkster's "retirement match." Hogan held the early edge until Papa Shango interfered, turning the tables for big Sid. It looked liked Hogan was going to lose until the Ultimate Warrior made an unexpected return to the WWF and interfered on Hogan's behalf, giving the Hulkster the victory.

Other matches at WrestleMania VIII were:

Owen Hart pinned Skinner

Natural Disasters beat Money Inc., Countout

Bret Hart defeated Roddy Piper for the Intercontinental title

The Undertaker pinned Jake Roberts

Virgil, Sgt. Slaughter, Jim Duggan, and the Big Boss Man defeated Repo Man, the Mountie, and the Nasty Boys via pinfall

WrestleMania VIII trivia: Before WrestleMania X8, this was Ric Flair's only WrestleMania appearance of his career!

WRESTLEMANIA IX, APRIL 4, 1993, CAESARS PALACE, LAS VEGAS, NV

Billed as the "World's Largest Toga Party," with singer Natalie Cole in a ringside seat, WrestleMania IX went down in the record books as the only time in Federation history that the World title changed hands twice in one day. And the man who emerged with the championship was totally unexpected as he hadn't even been scheduled for a title match!

The main event pitted champion Bret "The Hitman" Hart against the massive 500-pound-plus Yokozuna and it looked like he had the former sumo champ beaten. Applying his infamous finishing move, The Sharpshooter, Hart was stunned when Yokozuna's manager, Mr. Fuji, threw salt in his eyes. Yokozuna took advantage of the situation and pinned the blinded Hart to capture the title.

Hulk Hogan raced to Hart's aid and Fuji took the opportunity to challenge Hogan, putting Yokozuna's newly won title belt on the line. The injured Hart gave Hogan the go-ahead and, as the match commenced, Fuji resorted to his dirty tricks again and attempted to throw salt in Hogan's eyes. Fuji missed, however, blinding Yokozuna instead! Thinking quickly, Hogan seized the moment and pinned Yoko in under a minute to win his fifth WWF World title!

Other matches at WrestleMania IX were:

The Undertaker defeated Giant Gonzalez, DQ

Tatanka beat Shawn Michaels, DQ

Lex Luger pinned Mr. Perfect

The Steiners defeated the Headshrinkers via pinfall

Doink beat Crush via pinfall

Razor Ramon pinned Bob Backlund

Money Inc. defeated Hulk Hogan and Brutus Beefcake, DQ

WrestleMania IX trivia: For the occasion, ring announcer Howard Finkel's name was changed to "Finkus Maximus."

WRESTLEMANIA X, MARCH 20, 1994, MADISON SQUARE GARDEN, NEW YORK, NY

WrestleMania X brought wrestling fans back to where it all began ten years earlier, New York's Madison Square Garden. And fans were treated to the WWF's own version of "March Madness," as the WWF title was put on the line twice in one night, and featured what many consider to be the greatest WWF match of all time—the ladder match between Shawn Michaels and Razor Ramon.

The first title match saw WWF Champion Yokozuna defending his title against Lex Luger and the big man did indeed prevail, winning when Luger was disqualified by special guest referee Mr. Perfect. The second title match featured Yokozuna defending again against Bret Hart, who had been pinned by his younger brother, Owen, in the first match of the night. With Roddy Piper serving as a special guest referee, it was Bret, with an injured leg from his previous bout, in the final match of the night, who toughed it out to beat Yokozuna to capture the WWF World title.

Celebrities also were in the spotlight at WrestleMania X, with Cy Sperling, president of the Hair Club for Men, giving Howard Finkel a gift of a custom hairpiece; Donnie Wahlberg of New Kids On The

Block serving as a special ring announcer; Rhonda Shear, the host of USA Network's *Up All Night* serving as a guest timekeeper; actor Burt Reynolds serving as a special ring announcer; and actress Jennie Garth serving as a guest timekeeper.

A complete rundown of the WrestleMania X card is:

Owen Hart pinned Bret Hart

Bam Bam Bigelow and Luna beat Doink and Dink via pinfall

Randy Savage defeated Crush

Alundra Blayze defeated Leilani Kai

Men on a Mission beat the Quebecers, Countout

Yokozuna defeated Lex Luger, DQ

Earthquake pinned Adam Bomb

Razor Ramon defeated Shawn Michaels in a ladder match for the Intercontinental title

Bret Hart defeated Yokozuna for the WWF World title

WrestleMania X trivia: Tickets for WrestleMania X sold out so fast that it was also shown at the Paramount Theater next to Madison Square Garden on closed-circuit television.

WRESTLEMANIA XI, APRIL 2, 1995, HARTFORD CIVIC CENTER, HARTFORD, CT

WrestleMania XI was one of the most star-studded events in Federation history, with two main events and a host of celebrities in attendance, including rap stars Salt-n-Pepa, *Baywatch* star Pamela

Anderson, MTV's Jenny McCarthy, *Home Improvement* star Jonathan Taylor Thomas, *NYPD Blue* star Nicholas Turturro, and NFL stars Ken Norton, Jr., Carl Banks, Rickey Jackson, Steve McMichael, Reggie White, and Chris Spielman.

The title match pitted cocky Shawn Michaels against his former bodyguard, Diesel, for the WWF title. It was more than just a case of sour grapes as the two former allies waged war in the ring. Diesel kept the title after managing to floor the much smaller Michaels with a boot to the face and then stunning him with a Jackknife, setting him up for the pin.

Pride was also at stake in the other main event, in which Bam Bam Bigelow faced NFL great Lawrence Taylor. Bigelow had the backing of Ted DiBiase's Million Dollar Corporation while Taylor had his "All Pro Team" consisting of the aforementioned NFL stars, in his corner. Taylor stunned Bigelow with his football moves and a flying fist, pinning Bam Bam for the victory. The shamed Bigelow was duly drubbed out of the Corporation and was never the same in the ring again.

Other matches at WrestleMania XI were:

Bret Hart defeated Bob Backlund in an "I quit" match

Allied Forces beat Eli and Jacob Blu via pinfall

The Undertaker pinned King Kong Bundy

Owen Hart and Yokozuna defeated the Smoking Gunns for the Tag Team Championship

Razor Ramon defeated Jeff Jarrett, DQ

WrestleMania XI trivia: With Major League Baseball players on strike, American League umpire Larry Young served as referee for the match between The Undertaker and King Kong Bundy.

WRESTLEMANIA XII, MARCH 31, 1996, ARROWHEAD POND, ANAHEIM, CA

This year's WrestleMania extravaganza featured just six matches but for a good reason—the main event was a sixty-minute Iron Man match between Bret "The Hitman" Hart and Shawn Michaels. WrestleMania XII also lacked the usual crowd of celebrities, as the matches were so intense the WWF superstars were the only celebrities needed to generate excitement like never seen before.

With the WWF title on the line, Hart and Michaels engaged in the sport's most grueling match. In an Iron Man match, the wrestler who scores the most decisions via any method—pinfall, submission, countout, or disqualification—in sixty minutes is the winner. Michaels and Hart were so evenly matched that they went the distance to a full sixty minutes with neither able to force any decisions in the allotted time. WWF official Gorilla Monsoon put "sudden death" rules into effect to determine the winner and Michaels proved to be the better man this night, flooring Hart with a superkick and then pinning him to take Hart's title and begin living his boyhood dream of becoming WWF Champion! This was voted the fans' favorite WrestleMania match of all time in a WWF poll taken in 2000.

The other WrestleMania XII matches were:

The Ultimate Warrior defeated Hunter Hearst Helmsley via pinfall

Steve Austin defeated Savio Vega

Roddy Piper beat Goldust in a Backlot Brawl

The Undertaker pinned Diesel

Owen Hart, Vader, and Davey Boy Smith defeated Ahmed Johnson, Jake Roberts, and Yokozuna via pinfall

WrestleMania XII trivia: During the "Free for All" prior to WrestleMania XII, the WWF mocked some of their former superstars, when "The Huckster" took on the "Nacho Man" with "Billionaire Ted" serving as the guest referee.

WRESTLEMANIA 13, MARCH 23, 1997, ROSEMONT HORIZON, CHICAGO, IL

WrestleMania 13 emanated from the Windy City and was the second WrestleMania in history where the WWF superstars were the only celebrities on hand. The card was packed with rising stars such as The Undertaker and "Stone Cold" Steve Austin, as well as cagey veterans such as the Legion of Doom and Bret Hart.

In the main event, The Undertaker, who had previously held the WWF Championship briefly, was challenging the towering Sycho Sid for the prestigious title belt. His hunger to regain the belt was all-consuming and drove The 'Taker to finish off Sid with a Tombstone Piledriver and pin him to become WWF champ once again!

The other matches at WrestleMania 13 were:

The Legion of Doom and Ahmed Johnson defeated Crush, Faarooq, and Savio Vega in a Chicago Street Fight

Hunter Hearst Helmsley pinned Goldust

Bret Hart defeated Steve Austin in a submission match

The Headbangers defeated the Blackjacks, Furnas and Lafon, and the Godwins in a Four-Team Elimination match

Intercontinental Champion Rocky Maivia defeated the Sultan

Tag Team Champions Owen Hart and the British Bulldog vs. Mankind and Vader, Double Countout

WrestleMania 13 trivia: The Intercontinental title match saw Rocky Maivia take on the Sultan. The men, now known as The Rock and Rikishi Phatu, are still wrestling in the WWF and have gone on to superstar status!

WRESTLEMANIA XIV, MARCH 28, 1998, FLEET CENTER, BOSTON, MA

WrestleMania XIV featured one of the most anticipated main events in some time, as the feud between WWF head honcho Vince McMahon and "Stone Cold" Steve Austin reached fever pitch. McMahon was hoping his man Shawn Michaels would defeat Austin and, to ensure the outcome, he brought in Mike Tyson as a special referee and enforcer. Tyson appeared to be a fan of Michaels and D-Generation X, so the win seemed to be in the bag. As Austin and Michaels battled for the belt, however, Tyson showed his true colors—he was a "Stone Cold" fan! Austin naturally won the bout and his first WWF World Championship.

Celebrities returned to WrestleMania this year as boxers Vinny Pazienza and Marvin Hagler sat ringside, Gennifer Flowers interviewed The Rock and did some ring introductions, and baseball's all-time hit king Pete Rose received a Tombstone Piledriver from Kane. Rose apparently insulted the city of Boston one too many times as he did the ring introductions for the Kane vs. The Undertaker match.

Other matches at WrestleMania XIV were:

The Legion of Doom 2000 won a 15-Team Battle Royal

Taka Michinoku defeated Aguila in a Light-Heavyweight Championship match

Hunter Hearst Helmsley pinned Owen Hart in a European Championship match

Mark Mero and Sable defeated Goldust and Luna

The Rock beat Ken Shamrock via DQ in an Intercontinental Championship match

Cactus Jack and Chainsaw Charlie beat the New Age Outlaws in a dumpster match to win the Tag Team Championship

The Undertaker pinned Kane

WrestleMania XIV trivia: In his interview with Gennifer Flowers, The Rock used the phrase "if you smell what The Rock is cooking" for the first time!

WRESTLEMANIA XV, MARCH 28, 1999, FIRST UNION CENTER, PHILADELPHIA, PA

Called "The Ragin' Climax," WrestleMania XV was highlighted by a main event pitting WWF Champion The Rock against challenger "Stone Cold" Steve Austin. Still feuding with Austin, Vince McMahon appointed himself special referee for the match to guarantee a victory for The Rock. However, WWF Commissioner Shawn Michaels overruled and set up a regular WWF official to referee the bout. That official turned out to be none other than Mick Foley, otherwise known as the wrestler Mankind. The finish saw Austin lay out The Rock with a "Stone Cold" Stunner and pin him to win his third WWF Championship!

On hand for all the excitement were plenty of celebrities, including Pete Rose in a San Diego Chicken outfit; singers Isaac Hayes and Big Pun at ringside; and Mike Tyson's former trainer Kevin Rooney and ex-boxer Chuck Wepner as ringside judges.

The other matches at WrestleMania XV were:

Hardcore Holly defeated Al Snow and Billy Gunn to win the Hardcore Championship

The Undertaker defeated the Big Boss Man in a Hell in a Cell match

Tag Team Champions Owen Hart and Jeff Jarrett beat D'Lo Brown and Test

Shane McMahon pinned X-Pac

Butterbean defeated Bart Gunn in a Brawl for All

Sable pinned Tori

Mankind defeated The Big Show, DQ

Kane defeated Hunter Hearst Helmsley, DQ

The Road Dogg beat Ken Shamrock, Goldust, and Val Venis in a Four Corners
    Elimination Intercontinental Championship match

WrestleMania XV trivia: With his victory over The Rock, Steve Austin became the only man ever to win the WWF title at consecutive Wrestle-Manias.

WRESTLEMANIA 2000, APRIL 2, 2000, ARROWHEAD POND, ANAHEIM, CA

Getting in the spirit of the new millennium, the WWF added a new match to this year's WrestleMania. The main event was a Fatal Four-way for the World Wrestling Federation Championship, with a McMahon in the corner of each wrestler. Vince McMahon was in The Rock's corner, Stephanie McMahon was in the corner of her husband, the champion Hunter Hearst Helmsley and Shane McMahon was in the corner of The Big Show, while Linda McMahon coaxed Mick Foley to come out of retirement from his corner.

So it was that the McMahon family infighting became part of a WrestleMania main event. And what an event it was! Triple H hung on to his title but Vince, Shane, and Stephanie were all laid out by The Rock after the match was over, much to the delight of the crowd!

Pete Rose got into the WrestleMania action for the third time, attacking Kane but wound up getting chokeslammed by The Big Red Machine and then ended up on the wrong side of a Stinkface by Rikishi. Rapper Ice T provided a musical introduction for the Godfather and D'Lo Brown, and celebrities at ringside included *Third Rock from the Sun* star French Stewart, Oscar nominee Michael Clarke Duncan, TV and movie star Martin Short, and *Saved by the Bell* star Dustin Diamond.

The other matches at WrestleMania 2000 were:

The Big Boss Man and Bull Buchanan defeated the Godfather and D'Lo Brown

Kane and Rikishi defeated X-Pac and the Road Dogg

Hardcore Holly won a Hardcore Battle Royal to win the Hardcore title

Test and Albert beat Al Snow and Steve Blackman

Edge and Christian beat the Hardy Boyz and the Dudley Boyz in a "Tables, Ladders, and Chairs" match to win the Tag Team Championship

In a Triple Threat match for Kurt Angle's Intercontinental and European Championships, Chris Benoit pinned Chris Jericho to win the Intercontinental title and later Jericho defeated Benoit to win the European title

Terri defeated The Kat in a catfight

Too Cool and Chyna defeated Eddie Guerrero, Perry Saturn, and Dean Malenko

WrestleMania 2000 trivia: WrestleMania 2000 is the only WrestleMania ever not to feature a traditional one-on-one match.

WRESTLEMANIA X7, APRIL 1, 2001, ASTRODOME, HOUSTON, TX

A new attendance record was set at the Houston Astrodome as 67,925 fans, including Houston Astros Jeff Bagwell and Moises Alou, packed the venue to witness WrestleMania X7 and experience the thrill as "Stone Cold" Steve Austin pinned The Rock to become WWF Champion. Also on hand were the heavy metal group Motorhead, who played Triple H's theme before his match against The Undertaker. Unfortunately for Helmsley, he was pinned by The 'Taker, who upped his WrestleMania record to 9–0.

The other matches at WrestleMania X7 were:

Chris Jericho pinned William Regal in an Intercontinental title match

Tazz and APA defeated Right To Censor

Kane pinned The Big Show in a Hardcore title match

Eddie Guerrero pinned Test to become European Champion

Kurt Angle beat Chris Benoit via pinfall

Chyna pinned Ivory to become Women's Champion

Shane McMahon pinned Vince McMahon in a Streetfight

Edge and Christian beat the Hardy Boyz and the Dudley Boyz to become Tag Team Champions

The Iron Sheik won a Gimmick Battle Royal

WrestleMania X7 trivia: "Mean" Gene Okerlund and Bobby "The Brain" Heenan came to ringside to provide commentary for the Gimmick Battle Royal at WrestleMania X7.

WrestleMania certainly boasts an impressive history. So what's next for this cutting-edge annual extravaganza? Well, as we went to press, the WWF had announced that WrestleMania X8 was scheduled to take place March 17, 2002, at the SkyDome in Toronto, Ontario. "Only one city outside of the United States has been able to deliver WrestleMania to the world," said then–WWF President Stuart Snyder at a pep rally in Toronto's Nathan Phillips Square to announce the upcoming event. "Toronto was there for us in 1990 and we're very excited about making it our home again for WrestleMania X8."

An Axxess Fan Festival is scheduled for March 14–16 and the whole WrestleMania experience is being called the "Event of the Year" in Canada. But, then again, true wrestling fans know that in any given year, in any given location, WrestleMania is *always* the Event of the Year!

Wrestling Glossary

angle: a wrestling plot or story line

baby face: good guy

blade: the practice of cutting oneself in order to produce juice in a bout; a sharp object concealed by a wrestler in order to later draw blood

blow up: to become tired during a match

book: to schedule a wrestler for a card

booker: an individual in charge of many tasks like hiring, firing, match angles, and choosing the winners and losers

bump: to take a fall or move for your opponent's sake in a match

cage match: a bout that takes place in a ring that is surrounded by a steel cage

canned heat: artificial cheering or booing coming out of the arena sound system during a match

card: list of matches for an event

clean house: when a wrestler knocks off everyone in the ring

dark matches: untelevised matches

draw: wrestler who fans will pay to see; an outcome where there's no clear-cut winner

dud: bad or uninteresting match

face: good guy; baby face

fall: the end result after a referee's three-count with the loser's shoulders both touching the mat

finisher: a wrestler's key move that he/she usually uses to get the win

getting over: when a wrestler's gimmick is accepted by the fans

gimmick: character trait or traits that set wrestlers apart from one another

gold: championship belt

green: inexperienced wrestler who's still learning the ropes

hardway juice: to be legitimately cut during a match; can result from a shoot

heat: enthusiastic response to a heel's gimmick

heel: bad guy

highspot: high-risk maneuver

house: the wrestling audience

house show: a show not taped for TV

international object: a politically correct way of saying foreign or illegal object

jabroni: a loser; a jobber

job: to lose matches; a planned loss

jobber: a lesser-known or unknown wrestler whose main purpose is to lose matches, while helping make the more popular star look good

JTTS: jobber to the stars (usually a mid-card grappler)

juice: blood; also sometimes used as a reference to steroids

kayfabe: protecting the show; concealing the fake

mark: someone who thinks wrestling is real

paper: complimentary tickets

pencil: a promoter or booker

pop: energetic reaction from the crowd to a wrestler; rousing response to a wrestler's entrance

promotion: the wrestling federation

push: promoting a wrestler in order to get him/her over with the fans

resthold: a hold used by wrestlers to regain their energy during a match

rib: to play a joke on a wrestler

run-in: interference from an uninvolved wrestler

save: a run-in to protect a wrestler at the conclusion of his/her bout

screw job: a controversial finish to a match

sell (as in sell a move): make a foe's move look believable

shoot: real wrestling; opposite of work

sleeper: a common resthold

smart: a fan who knows everything about wrestling; an in-the-know rooter

spot: a particular segment of a match; usually the high point

squash: when a wrestler totally dominates his foe in a match

stable: a group of united wrestlers

stiff: a hit or move that can cause real harm; not an adroit wrestler

strap: championship belt

submission hold: a lethal and painful maneuver that usually makes the receiver tap out or give in

tag team: a wrestling duo

tap-out: when a wrestler concedes to his foe by repeatedly tapping the mat during a painful hold to indicate to the ref and his foe that he/she has had enough

TLC match: death-defying match where tables, ladders, and chairs are present in the ring for the bout

to post: to drive an opponent's head into the turnbuckle

Triple Threat match: three wrestlers square off at the same time in the ring

turn: a change in a wrestler's personality (good guy to bad guy or vice versa)

tweener: a wrestler who is neither heel nor face; may be in the process of a turn

work: a staged event or occurrence that seems legit